AF572552

Worrying About Race
1985-1995

Worrying About Race 1985-1995:

Reflections During a Troubled Time

Sanford Pinsker

The Whitston Publishing Company
Troy, New York
1996

Copyright 1996
Sanford Pinsker

Library of Congress Catalog Card Number 95-61176

ISBN 0-87875-474-1

Printed in the United States of America

To the memory of Peter Shaw (1937-1995):
mentor, confidante, and friend.

Acknowledgments

Author and publisher wish to thank the following publications for allowing us to reproduce articles and reviews by Sanford Pinsker which appeared previously in these publications, sometimes in a slightly different form: *Reconstruction, The Virginia Quarterly Review, The Georgia Review,* and the *Jewish Exponent.*

Contents

Introduction

Worrying About Race represents a collection of, well, my "worries," ones that I suspect many others—black and white alike—have been secretly sharing during the past decades. Race dominates the American agenda as few topics do, but it is a difficult subject to worry about publicly and all the more so if the worrier in question happens to be white. I am, of course, the worrier I am speaking of, and the essays and reviews that follow represent a continuing (and I hope, honest) effort to confront our worsening racial situation with the seriousness and honesty it deserves. Little will be served by once again rehearsing the long trail of tears that has brought us to our present predicament or by so overemphasizing white empathy that every failure of black responsibility is laid at history's altar.

At the same time, I write as one who was formed in the crucible of the civil rights struggle. Indeed, long before I would have identified the cause in the shape and form that Martin Luther King, Jr. provided, I somehow knew in my very bones that the patterns of segregation that existed just north of the Mason-Dixon line were horribly wrong. Here I speak of small-town life as it was in Washington, Pennsylvania, a mill town some twenty-eight miles from Pittsburgh. If the deep South struck the average Washingtonian as "another country"—so foreign were its odd customs as a land soundly, and rightly, defeated in the Civil War—it did not strike that same citizen as peculiar that blacks sat in the balcony when they ponied up their money to see a movie (there were, unlike the South, no signs directing them to this balcony; it was simply understood by all that this is where "they" were to go) or that the town sported separate but unequal municipal swimming pools or YMCAs.

The Christmas season was particularly troubling (perhaps I should say "worrying") because it was then that the "white" Y hosted an annual party to which members of the "black" Y were invited. As I remember it, everybody joined in song and games, in refreshments and fellowship, in an auditorium that sported posters of children of all colors dancing in the ring. What bothered me was that when the party was over and the posters replaced by next month's theme, each constituency returned to its respective quarters. I am still bothered by that memory, in something of the way that Abraham Lincoln was forever affected by the specters of slavery he witnessed as a young man.

Small wonder, then, that I have not been heartened by the reemergence of "voluntary" segregation, whether it be in all-black college dormitories (almost always justified with the rubric of "theme houses") or a growing sense among many blacks that "white America" is neither their land nor destiny. For one thing, I know too much about black history to believe such drivel (if anything, blacks contributed greatly to the America I now enjoy); for another, the democratic promises that mean so much to me as a Jewish-American suggest quite another vision.

The essays and reviews that follow may focus on a wide variety of subjects, but, taken together, they sound remarkably similar themes: that our intellectual debate about race needs to be sharpened, both by way of rigorous critique and candor; that our leadership must move beyond sound bites and political jockeying to more fully address the economic conditions that foster despair and ultimately suicidal behaviors; that black rage and white backlash must be replaced by an honest recognition of difference as well as an equally honest recognition of the areas of common cause that bind us together as Americans.

To all these "worries," I add yet another, for *writing* about race is akin to negotiating a minefield. Dangers lurk on the other side of every comma, every semi-colon. Indeed, there are times when the discretion of silence seems the better part of valor. But attractive as writing about other matters might have been, the bald truth is that I found myself returning, again and again, to the vexing, worrying business of race. In short, I can say of this subject what I often remark about my poems—namely, that it—and they—choose me, rather than the other way around.

Worrying can, of course, become an end unto itself but I hope that this is not the case here, for as I cobbled slightly older pieces with newer ones I discovered a unity of purpose that was not apparent "in-progress." My fondest wish is that readers will also notice the vision underlying these disparate pieces, and more important, that they will serve as a basis for the "worrying"—and serious reflection—we all need to do about the long national nightmare that has stained our history and darkened our horizon for far too long.

He Had a Dream, and It Shot Him: What Happened to Visions of Racial Harmony, and Why

As Huckleberry Finn puts it, in an effort to explain how Tom got himself wounded during the chaos following Jim's "evasion": "he had a dream, and it shot him." One could say much the same thing about Twain himself; he had a wonderful dream in which an ignorant, fourteen-year-old white boy and an adult slave float down the Mississippi, only to find themselves lost in the fog, run over by a steamboat, and forced to share their Edenic world with con men. Granted, lessons are learned, understanding happened, but the towns along the shore, and the people who inhabited them, cannot be dismissed with a wave of one's hand. For all its highjinks and humor, the world of *Adventures of Huckleberry Finn* is a tough, heart-cracking place.

Dreams, of course, come with the American territory. Indeed, they are a defining feature of our history as well as our psychic landscape. Small wonder, then, that John Winthrop's vision of the new American Jerusalem (what his words aboard the *Arabella* called a "cittie on the hill") blend so seamlessly with the final paragraphs of F. Scott Fitzgerald's *The Great Gatsby* or the cadences of Martin Luther King, Jr.'s "I Have a Dream" speech.

That we have seen aspects of the "dream" turn materialistic and then greedy is true enough; but the larger, better vision persists—partly because it promises to close the gap between democratic promise and a compromised reality, partly because the eloquent words of our Declaration of Independence—propped as they are on principles of freedom and equality—still defines our nation at its best.

Among W. E. B. DuBois's most quoted remarks is his worry that the color line would emerge as *the* problem of the twentieth century. He had the elaborate tapestry of Jim Crow segregation in mind, although one might argue that other nightmares ultimately defined our century: the Holocaust precipitated by Nazism, the Stalinesque gulags, the specter of nuclear annihilation, and a host of other threats—environmental, economic, social, and civic—that continue to sound ugly alarms. Still, for Americans, race remains a significant shadow. One thinks, for example, of another nineteenth-century American writer—Herman Melville—who worried about race in ways that cannot fail to strike us as prophetic. Unlike Twain, Melville's "baggage" was a brooding Calvinism stripped of its theological underpinning—a revisionist version of Original Sin, if you will, but one that continued to insist on sinfulness as a palpable human reality. In this regard he differed sharply with giddy transcendentalists such as Emerson and Thoreau; and in "Benito Cereno," he used the occasion of a rebellion on a slave ship to test out not only the warring claims of illusion and reality, but also the effects of slavery on an individual psyche. Don Amaso Delano, the thickheaded, altogether innocent American captain, cannot see the mutiny before his very eyes just as, later, he cannot fathom the shadow that hangs eternally over Benito Cereno. "You are saved," he insists—this after the life-threatening rebellion has been crushed. Why, then, is his Spanish counterpart in such a funk? "What has cast over you?" he wonders. Benito Cereno's reply is instructive: "The negro"; and for my purposes it stands as yet another twist on Huck Finn's quip about dreams that end by shooting the dreamer.

In the decades since the apparent triumphs of the Civil Rights Movement, we have found ourselves in conditions that force us to ruminate on the similarities between earlier American dreamers and ourselves. Perhaps no statement about the great dream of racial justice was more eloquent, more moving than Martin Luther King, Jr.'s words uttered at the Lincoln Memorial on August 28, 1963: "I have a dream that my four children will one day live in a nation where they will not be judged by the color of their skin, but by the content of their character."

To be sure, King's speech was a laundry list of "dreams," orchestrated in litanies and delivered with the full throat of Southern Baptist oratory at its best. He dreamed, for example, of the day when the sons of slaves and the sons of slaveholders would be able to sit down together at the table of brotherhood, when the stains of the past would at last be washed clean by the collective will of good people of every color and condition. Justice, he insisted, would then run like a mighty river.

Remembering that day, that speech, I was hardly alone in feeling that our nation had turned an important corner—only to realize, a few decades later, that the ugly shadow Melville's character pointed toward had arrived. But, then, again, none of us in the innocence of 1963 could have imagined the ingenious spin that deconstructionists could put on King's words, much less the widespread disenchantment with his integrationist vision. As the poet W. H. Auden points out in his elegy to William Butler Yeats, the words of the dead are "modified in the guts of the living." Much the same thing could be said of King's pronouncements.

Here, for example, is literary critic Stanley Fish's *take*, his calculated "misreading," if you will, of the most famous line of King's most famous speech. To judge blacks by the "content of their character" rather than by the "color of their skin" is to lie down with mighty strange bedfellows. What, Fish wonders, would King say about David Duke's claim that "What we want in this country is equal opportunity for everyone, not affirmative action for a few" or about those who pepper their prose with phrases like "colorblind" or "race-neutral"? Haven't they, in fact, turned the eloquent words King uttered from the steps of the Lincoln Memorial into "coded" (Fish's word) messages that are transparent, easy to crack, and end up saying pretty much the same thing—namely, that "Those niggers and kikes and faggots have come far enough; it's time to stop them before they take our jobs, cheat our children out of a place in college, and try to move in next door"?

As Fish's argument would have it, the same reservations one (rightly) has about David Duke should be logically extended to anybody raising a question about affirmative action and entitlement programs (presumably including Shelby Steele, whose *The Content of Our Character* meditates on King's speech in quite different ways from Fish), to anyone lacking a proper enthusiasm for multiculturalist curricula, and finally, to anyone with the slightest concern about the *unum* in *e pluribus unum*. Find yourself in any of these camps and you will discover that Fish writes you off as a racist. Indeed, this is precisely what happened to Arthur Schlesinger, Jr. when he had the gall to act as the professional historian he is, and to suggest not only that Enlightenment thinkers (white European males, every last one of them) had more to do with the framing of the Declaration of Independence and the Constitution than did the Iroquois Confederation, but also that the more insistent demands of multiculturalists threaten to tear the national fabric into balkanized shreds.

No matter that Fish lacks the scholarly distinction, to say nothing of the sociopolitical track record, of an Arthur Schlesinger, Jr., and no matter that there are worlds of difference between the xenophobes of the past whom Fish cites and the Schlesinger he attacks, the plain truth is that Fish means to play as dirty as he has to to tarnish Schlesinger's reputation and to tar his arguments. After surveying Lawrence Auster's *The Path to National Suicide*, Richard Brookhiser's *The Way of the Wasp*, and Schlesinger's *The Disuniting of America*, Fish comes to this conclusion:

> What does it all mean? Does it suggest that Auster, Brookhiser, and Schlesinger are racists? Well, if you mean by racist someone who actively seeks the subjugation of groups thought inferior to his own, none of these qualify. If you mean by racist someone whose views about race, if acted upon in political ways, will lead to the disadvantaging of certain groups, then Mr. Auster is a serious candidate; and if you mean by racism the deployment of a vocabulary that avoids racist talk but has the effect of perpetuating racial stereotypes and the institutions that promote them, then Mr. Brookhiser is in the running; and Mr. Schlesinger, with his talk of the inevitable Anglo-Saxon "coloration" of the American character and the necessity of sublimating ethnic strains in true American amalgam, is a shoo-in.

No doubt Mr. Fish means what he says when he calls Schlesinger a racist (no rhetorical ploys or recontextualizations here), and at a certain point one begins to wonder if King himself would be spared the lash of his self-righteous indignation. After all, King's talk about the "content of their character" has been enormously troubling, because, slice it as you will, his words make it clear that people are more than the arithmetic of their race, class, and gender; and furthermore, that they should be judged by the moral force of the *more*. That idea, then and now, strikes me as one worth fighting for, however much it may be shamelessly exploited by David Duke and others like him. Indeed, King's words are best understood as part of a long American tradition that values the individual and places enormous emphasis on his or her democratic freedoms.

Fish obviously feels otherwise, and he is so worried about the appropriations that have surrounded the two parts of King's parallelism—skin color on one side of the equation, character on the other—that he is obligated, even compelled, to reconstitute, even to "deconstruct," the words I heard on that hot afternoon of 1963 and that have been echoing in my mind ever since. In Fish's case, the result is everything that is unworthy and dangerous in the current theoretical fascination with making words mean whatever suits the purpose;

> I am not saying [Fish begins] that Martin Luther King would have wanted his children to be judged by the color of their skin, as if that were in and of itself an entitlement; but neither would he have wanted the color of their skin to be wholly irrelevant to the determination of what they had to offer to society. He says to those he addresses in 1963, "You have been the veterans of creative suffering." That is, the strength you here display by participating in this march is the product of your trials in the face of racism; and it is by virtue of those trials that you have become what you are, veterans of a war whose terms you did not choose. King salutes his followers not because their skins are black but because the blackness of their skins has generated the experience that has tempered them. In short, *the color of their skin has in some measure been the content of their character*. (Emphasis in original)

Small wonder that people throw up their hands and roll their eyeballs when Fish turns plain sense, and plainer language, on its head. Appeals to reason—or for that matter to evidence—count for precious little because only liberals continue to keep faith that "reason" (the term is now surrounded by inverted commas and made to look mighty suspicious) operates independently of any particular worldview. What this means, Fish argues, is that "not all reasons (or reasonable trains of thought) are reasons for everyone." So, while I think it reasonable (the hell with inverted commas) that Dr. King meant precisely what he said in his "I have a Dream" speech, Fish would insist that such a reading merely reflects something about my worldview and, in this case, probably reveals I was a racist fellow even during the days when I was in the ranks at his marches. And as for evidence to support his curious "misreading" of King's motivations—evidence from, say, King's public writings or private papers—apparently none is necessary. What matters for Fish is the political objective closest at hand, and to further its cause you make language, as they say, "work for you."

To cite a very different example, Malcolm X also knew how to make language work for him. His in-your-face, often inflammatory rhetoric made it abundantly clear that separatism was preferable to King's dream of integration. There are, to be sure, a dizzying array of Malcolms (the street hustler and criminal, the charismatic disciple of Elijah Mohammed, as well as the man who was assassinated because his dream of pan-African brotherhood ran afoul of the Nation of Islam's sociopolitical orthodoxies), and it is fair to say that myth-making plays an active role in each incarnation. We isolate the Malcolm X who speaks to our deepest dreams, whether they be of militant separatism or universal brotherhood. All of which is to admit that the debates about legacies—Martin Luther King, Jr. vs. Malcolm X—will probably continue to rage across the generational divide: the young identifying with Malcolm's revolutionary postures while those who vividly remember what segregated life was like *before* King will retain a faith (no doubt punctuated by bouts of skepticism and even pockets of despair) in the less romantic business of mainstream politics.

To talk about Malcolm X is to talk about *everything*—which, of course, is also to talk about nothing. For example, is he primarily the iconic figure whose X adorned baseball caps in the hoopla that once surrounded Spike Lee's epical film, the philosopher king solemnly studied in a wide variety of academic classes, or simply one more example of a black longer on charisma than sound sense? Let me focus, instead, on a single moment, one that predates our current fascination with the "sound bite," but that serves to illustrate both the raw power of his oratory and the disastrous consequences it could have. During one of his visits to Harvard during the early 1970s, Malcolm posed the following question: "What do you call a black man with a Ph.D.?" The answer, one clearly designed to cut through Ivy League pretension, was "A nigger." That his no nonsense, tell-it-as-it-is quip shocked the assemblage is true enough (one might even argue that a certain amount of cutting through the bullshit was called for), but the effect, then and now, was to suggest that educational achievement—yea, even education itself—was as threadbare as it was bogus. And this at the very school that provided W. E. B. DuBois with what he called "the freedom of the library and laboratories," and more important, the opportunities that that education afforded.

Whatever the feel-good advantages of Malcolm X's remark might be, they amount to precious little when stacked against the sobering realities of life in an increasingly complicated world. And it is here that the very different educational dreams of Booker T. Washington and W. E. B. DuBois—the former aimed at vocational training, the latter at the intellectual cultivation of a "talented tenth"—turn into nightmare, for if the Malcolm X who stuck it to Harvard's black professors is right, black youngsters would be well advised to give higher learning the raspberry it richly deserves.

Here, there is much to worry about—not only in the chilling statistic that shows more young black males in prison than in college classrooms, but also in reports suggesting that college students in general read more books during their undergraduate years than they read throughout the rest of their lives. In short, this is at once a black problem and an American dilemma, for the hard truths about international competition are inextricably linked to any reasonable hope that racial tensions will be reduced and something amounting to racial harmony will be achieved. What Jefferson recognized long ago—namely, that democracy itself depends on an educated, enlightened citizenry—is even truer today. What do you call a black man with a Ph.D.? I should hope that the answer would be self-evident: Professor, nothing more but certainly nothing less. Indeed, I would argue that this is as self-evident as are our inalienable American rights to life, liberty, and the pursuit of happiness.

No doubt the Malcolm X who uncorked his zinger at Harvard would insist that America always was, and remains to this day, a racist country rather than a country with a certain distressing quotient of racists. At this point I realize full well that my quarrel with Malcolm is about perception, but the sheer fact that the black middle class is, in Daniel Patrick Moynihan's words, "doing quite nicely" belies many of Malcolm's confident assumptions. Educational opportunity has surely played an important role in the equation, just as the despair of the black underclass continues to worry all persons with an inclination toward social justice.

Much of Malcolm X's dream was wrapped in the folds of the loopy mythology and militantly separatist rhetoric of the Nation of Islam. In his case, it is safe to say that this was a dream which shot him—quite literally—every bit as much as Twain's dream of an easy, unencumbered dream of racial harmony floundered on the rocks of anti-bellum reality. Add Stokley Carmichael's 1967 call for "Black Power!" and the result is a world in which well-meaning whites need no longer apply for positions in the ongoing struggle for black self-determination. Here, an ad once run by the United Negro College Fund may prove instructive. It featured a classroom in which black students are told that because the college has run out of money, it has been forced to close. The camera zooms in on one student who is especially distressed, as we watch his face move by increments from shock to anger, and then to rage. The theme of the fund-raising campaign is "A mind is a terrible thing to waste," but its sub-text is a less than subtle reminder that young blacks are as bloodthirsty and savage as the ugly stereotype would have it. One feels something of the same spirit in placards that there will be "no peace" if there is "no justice."

Carmichael's dream of black power has been longer on encouraging blacks to reject mainstream politics and the large American commonweal than it has been on tangible results. If the decades since the passage of the Civil Rights Act have been disappointing, what can one say of the years since the clenched black fist, raised toward the heavens, has been a fact of public life? Is this not yet another instance of a dream that boomerangs? For there is a large difference between what generates media ink and what effectively alters quotidian conditions. In the case of black power, it is forever scouring what it rejects (in Carmichael's words, "racist institutions and the values of this society"), and pointing toward the unified black consciousness it has yet to bring into being. Meanwhile, the beat of racial division, that long national nightmare we have yet to fully awaken from, goes on.

Leadership, in short, has been a continuing problem, not only in terms of the vacuum left by Martin Luther King, Jr.'s death, but also in American politics generally. The relentless assault on American institutions—whether the result of the ascendancy of postmodernist "theory" or simply a fin de siècle malaise—has taken an enormous toll on formerly stable entities. And while the plaint about America's decline-and-fall is at once too easy and often exaggerated, who can deny the palpable realities of drugs and urban crime, our shirking economic base or national mood of unfocused anger? Those who care not a fig for poetry know W. B. Yeats's line about the center no longer holding, and nod their heads in agreement.

Meanwhile, race relations—bad at the moment, and threatening to become much, much worse—exacerbate what can only be called a bad patch. Small wonder, then, that I found myself drawn to the following paragraph from *Daydreams and Nightmares*, Irving Louis Horowitz's remarkable memoir of growing up Jewish in an increasingly black Harlem:

> The experience of Harlem convinced me that the relationship of blacks and Jews in America has special historical significance. This is not to make fatuous claims about harmony and common cause; rather, to assert that these two distinctly different peoples—sometimes marching arm in arm as in the civil rights struggle, other times in bitter confrontation as in Bedford-Stuyvesant—tell us much about the moral status of the nation at any given moment in time. They tell a story of aspirations realized and thwarted, cultures transmitted yet bowdlerized, and groups seeking security in race or religious solidarity up against individuals seeking to escape the boundaries of group life as such.

As my admittedly selective examples show, Mark Twain was hardly alone in spinning out a dream that shot him. And while I suspect that others could provide countless examples of the same phenomenon, my point is that race is likely to be at the center. For too long now race has been *the* taboo subject, the topic that most frequently occasions paralysis, and then an uneasy silence. Better to dummy up than to risk even the appearance of insensitivity much less the heavier charge of being a racist. There are, however, signs that the times are a'changin'. One of them is the national debate over affirmative action that may, just may, move beyond the opportunism of presidential politics and the sound-biting it encourages. Another is Dinesh D'Souza's *The End of Racism*, a thick, meticulously researched book which argues that if racism has an identifiable point of origin, it can also have an ending. His analysis, as well as his conclusions, are not likely to go unchallenged (indeed, I can imagine readers quarreling with virtually every one of its 700 pages), but what finally matters is a significant change in how we conduct our ongoing debate about race. For we have gone about as far as a shouting match pitting black rage against white backlash can take us. Too much is at stake—for the nation and more important, for our national dream of liberty and justice—to postpone honest talk any longer. We cannot live our lives on a raft, floating wherever the river might take us, but we must find ways to bring what we stand for and what we are into congruence. Too many people—black and white, men and women—have given their very lives to this endeavor for those of us who enjoy the dream's many blessings to do less.

America's Conspiratorial Imagination

> That's the struggle of humanity, to recruit others to your version of what's real.
>
> —Augie March

Depending on to whom you listen, the American economy is either temporarily stalled or headed down the slippery slope, but nobody, absolutely *nobody*, doubts that conspiracy theory is a sure-fire money-maker. Indeed, for those who specialize in new installments of "Who Shot JFK?," conspiracy-spinning is a growth industry and this is a boom time. One thinks, for example, of recent books such as Mark Lane's *Plausible Denial*, along with a paperback reprinting of his pioneering *Rush to Judgment*; Charles A. Crenshaw's *JFK: Conspiracy of Silence*; Jim Marrs' *Crossfire: The Plot that Killed Kennedy*; Jim Garrison's *On the Trail of the Assassins*; and Harrison Edward Livingstone's *High Treason 2*. For those who prefer their paranoia on the silver screen, there is always Oliver Stone's *JFK*, knock-offs like *Ruby*, and, no doubt, a half-dozen other docu-dramas about what *really* happened on Nov. 22, 1963 being hatched up as I keyboard this sentence.

Small wonder, then, that it's not hard to imagine the day when "Shots Heard 'Round the World: From Concord Bridge to Dealey Plaza" will finally replace "From Beowulf to Virginia Woolf" as the survey title of choice. What worries me about this is not that one student-grabbing gimmick gives way to another, but rather that we no longer believe, as Emerson once did, in the possibility of public events being transmogrified into public poetry. Instead, we have increasingly private "takes" on reality itself, each more conspiratorial than the last and all of them dedicated to the proposition that official histories "lie" and that only alternative versions tell the truth.

Granted, no term is slipperier, more hotly debated, or

more important than *reality*. As such, Saul Bellow's *The Adventures of Augie March* (1953) is a case study in what its larky protagonist calls "the struggle of humanity"—namely, how others try to recruit him to their version of the real, and how he manages to squirm out of their respective clutches. Augie is, at one and the same time, eminently "adoptable" (a fact that does not go unnoticed by a wide range of would-be benefactors) and inclined toward "opposition." Indeed, one could say the same things about Bellow himself. In an age where "brutal realism" strikes many as the only brand worthy of serious attention, Bellow's fiction has, in effect, answered the question he first posed in *Dangling Man* (1944)—namely, "What in all this [decaying urban landscape] speaks for man?"

Granted, Bellow is a special case, not only because he is the only 20th-century American novelist who deserves mention in the same breath with William Faulkner, but also because he is one of the few contemporary American writers unafraid to use the word "soul." However much Bellow anchors his fiction in the quotidian world, his inner eye remains fastened on airier, more transcendental realms. He has, in short, a decidedly mystical bent, one that unleashes great imaginative power, but that turns reality itself into the problematic. What, for example, is one to make of Augie's insistence that the real world is simultaneously self-evident and unseen?

> Everyone tries to create a world he can live in, and what he can't use he often can't see. But the real world is already created, and if your fabrication doesn't correspond, then even if you feel noble and insist on there being something better than what people call reality, that better something needn't try to exceed what, in its actuality, since we know it so little, may be very surprising.

Other writers have defined the "surprises" that life throws at artists rather differently. For example, a young whippersnapper named Philip Roth put the matter this way in a 1961 essay entitled "Writing American Fiction":

> . . . the American writer in the middle of the twentieth century has his hands full in trying to understand, describe, and then make credible much of American reality. It stupifies, it sickens, it infuriates, and finally it is even a kind of embarrassment to one's own meager imagination. The actuality is continually outdoing our talents, and the culture tosses up figures almost daily that are the envy of any novelist. Who, for example, could have invented Charles Van Doren? Roy Cohn and

> David Schine? Sherman Adams and Bernard Goldfine? Dwight David Eisenhower?

Roth, of course, had burst onto the scene with *Goodbye, Columbus* (1959), a collection that gave social realism a suburban, Jewish-American twist and that earned its 26-year-old author a National Book Award. Granted, he took a certain amount of drubbing from those not amused by his satiric portraits of gold-bricking Jewish soldiers ("Defender of the Faith") or adulterous Jewish fathers ("Epstein"), but those with an ear knew better. Here was a new, exciting *voice*, one that a subsequent Roth character would describe as "something that begins at around the back of the knees and reaches well above the head." Who better, then, to pontificate about the state of contemporary writing in the early 1960's—especially since Roth was so good at what he called "reading himself & others"?

That his remarks about American reality and the individual American writer were much-quoted (indeed, that they helped to shape our critical agenda for nearly two decades) is now universally regarded as a cultural fact. And this *before* the days when novelists must have scratched their heads and wondered which of them could have invented Tiny Tim? Spiro Agnew? Richard Nixon?—much less the likes of Donald Trump, Ivan Boesky, or Al Sharpton! Indeed, however much Tom Wolfe might boast about the ways that *The Bonfire of the Vanities* (1987) had taken on material most American novelists shy away from—either because they lack his journalistic skill or his artistic courage—the fact of the matter is that even *Wolfe's* novel did not prepare us for Tawana Brawley's tale of abduction and denigration, much less for the sad spectacle of her systematic exploitation when the "story" collapsed under the sheer weight of its desperation and calculated duplicity.

Still, "Stalking the Billion-Footed Beast," Wolfe's wholesale attack on contemporary American fiction, knew how to make a literary splash. It had all the advantages of good timing and even better connections, of large, cheeky generalizations and even a few grains of truth. Consider, for example, these snippets from what the editors at *Harper's* subtitled as "A Literary Manifesto for the New Social Novel":

> After the Second World War, in the late 1940s, American intellectuals began to revive a dream that had glowed briefly in the 1920s. They set out to create a native intelligentsia on the French or English model, an intellectual aristocracy—socially unaffiliated, be-

> yond class distinctions—active in politics and the arts. In the arts, their audience would be the inevitably small minority of truly cultivated people as opposed to the mob, who wished only to be entertained or to be assured they were "cultured." By now, if one need edit, the mob was better known as the middle class.
>
> The lesson that a generation of serious young writers learned from Roth's lament [in "Writing American Fiction"] was that it was time to avert their eyes. To attempt a realistic novel with the scope of Balzac, Zola, or Lewis was absurd. By the mid-1960s the conviction was not merely that the realistic novel was no longer possible but that American life itself no longer deserved the term. American life was chaotic, fragmented, random, discontinuous; in a word, *absurd*. Writers in university creative writing programs had long, phenomenological discussions in which they decided that the act of writing words on a page was the real thing and the so-called real world of America was the fiction, requiring the suspension of disbelief. *The so-called real world* became a favorite phrase.

That Wolfe means to put forth *The Bonfire of the Vanities* as the Big Social Novel no contemporary American writer can match is clear enough; but self-promotion aside, was there anything in his critique worthy of serious attention? I think so, even as I would insist that there are mighty distinctions to be made between the social landscaping of, say, a Dickens or a Balzac and the thin gruel served up in Wolfe's saga of how Sherman McCoy bit the urban dust. For one thing, Wolfe was dead right about those times, those places that gave birth to what John Barth once called "the literature of exhaustion." During the mid-sixties, experiments in radical reflexivity, in fiction about its own fictionality, seemed dazzling stuff indeed. Most of us did not realize, however, that a subtle shift in the collective literary sensibility was taking place under our very noses.

What Randall Jarrell, with at least as much misgiving as description, identified as the Age of Criticism (more or less the "age" in which I first encountered formalism and learned to think of irony, paradox, myth, and symbol as the stuff of which well-wrought urns are made)—was slowly transforming itself—without ambivalence, without irony, and certainly without the slightest trace of humor—into the Age of Theory. I would like to count myself among those acolytes of Joyce and Eliot, of Hemingway and Faulkner, who would have given "theory" the bum's rush in the 1970s, but the bald fact is that theory, like

Sandburg's fog, crept in on cat's feet and wearing a collar marked "post-modernism." No matter that the term was, let us say, imprecise, or that it signaled a generalized cultural attitude rather than an entity one could point to—yea, even touch—like the great monuments of literary modernism; what mattered in those days was the giddy sense of release from all that had been established, domesticated in undergraduate classrooms, in a word, *canonized*.

II

That solemn, increasingly unreadable books about postmodernist experimentation continue to be written and published is true enough, but the phenomenon strikes me as more a comment on academic inertia than on our cultural condition. For the hot competition these days is one that divides those who retain a measure of allegiance to social reality and those who dismiss "reality" itself as yet another instance of the conspiratorial fog. In this sense, Roth's manifesto about the dizzying nature of American reality has been replaced by a widely shared view that one conspiracy or another *is* the reality. I have in mind not only evidence from the arts—everything from *V* (1963), Thomas Pynchon's first novel, to Oliver Stone's film, *JFK* (1991)—but also the rising star of conspiracy theory itself.

Kafka turned his world into mystery. By contrast, many contemporary writers are predisposed to explanation. And Roth, then and now, is hardly shy when it comes to justifying how and why he happened to write books such as *Portnoy's Complaint* or the Zuckerman chronicles. Interestingly enough, for the patient, meticulous E. I. Lonoff of *The Ghost Writer*, a life of "turning sentences around" is sufficient. He need not explain, much less defend, the work that has brought a younger, less confident Nathan Zuckerman to his door. But as Lonoff also points out, a writer of Zuckerman's temperament requires a more turbulent life. The Zuckerman chronicles are a record of that turbulence, full of the sound, the fury, and the exclamation points that signify the Jewish-American writer's essentially misunderstood condition:

> Not everybody was delighted by this book [*Carnovsky*] that was making Zuckerman a fortune. Plenty of people had already written to tell him off. "For depicting the Jews in a peep-show atmosphere of total perversion, for

> depicting Jews in acts of adultery, exhibitionism, masturbation, sodomy, fetishism, and whoremongery," somebody with a letterhead stationery as impressive as the President's had even suggested that he "ought to be shot." And in the spring of 1969 this was no longer just an expression. . . . Oh Madam, if only you knew the real me! Don't shoot! I am a serious writer as well as one of the boys!

What Zuckerman craves, of course, is sympathy, but his spirited defense is also a mirror held up to the nature of American reality, albeit one filtered through Zuckerman's admittedly wounded sensibility. What, after all, is Alvin Pepler, the Jewish marine snookered out of his 15 minutes of quiz show fame, if not a profile in paranoia, yet another instance of conspiracy theory-as-reality? Granted, *Zuckerman Unbound* makes it abundantly clear that while Pepler may be a comic character, he is hardly a reliable witness; but can one say the same for similar characters in novels by Thomas Pynchon or Don DeLillo? Here we are meant to take the loopiest readings of history as simultaneously outrageous and darkly "true." More important, where is "American reality" amid the charges and counter-charges that collect around everything from UFOs to AIDS, and that have been piling up since that fateful day in Dallas when President Kennedy was shot? Poor Zuckerman makes his way through the lunacy that is America 1950-1990, often turning whole lives, rather than Lonovian sentences, around in an effort to see the culture both steady and whole.

Nearly 30 years ago Richard Hofstadter identified the general impulse I've been addressing as "The Paranoid Style in American Politics." By "paranoid style," Hofstadter meant to grab a term from clinical psychology and apply it, "much as a historian of art might speak of the baroque and of expressionist style," as a way of describing how an increasing number of people on the radical right see the world. To be sure, the overheated suspicions of the clinical paranoid insist that the machinations of a hostile, conspiratorial world are directed against *him*; by contrast, spokesmen of the paranoid style argue that the plot "out there" is aimed at the culture at large, against the nation as a whole and the very fabric of life all right-thinking people hold dear. In this way Hofstadter meant to call attention to the "qualities of heated exaggeration, suspiciousness, and conspiratorial fantasy" that clustered around a number of bad causes (e.g., opposition to community fluoridation projects or gun control legislation), and that spawned the likes of Joseph McCarthy, the John Birch Society, and the Goldwater movement.

Given the sheer range of conspiracy theorists, both right and left, in the years since Hofstadter first called our attention to the paranoid style, a reassessment strikes me as appropriate. My interest is directed less toward the strictly "political" aspects of Hofstadter's thesis than to why America itself has proved so congenial to the paranoid style. And here I think our unique situation as a self-created land, as a concoction of myth as much as of history, deserves emphasis.

For we are not only the inheritors of everything our Puritan forbears packed into bracing phrases such as "a city upon a hill" or the "New Jerusalem," but also of a Manichean vision that ascribes as much force to the powers of darkness as to those of light. In short, good and evil have *always* grappled for the American soul; and it may well be that that pitched battle is as accurate a way of describing the American sensibility as any. It is hardly an accident, therefore, that our classic writers were drawn to images of America as the New Eden or that "Adam" emerged as the quintessential American character; nor should it seem surprising that our greatest writers had differing views about our perfectability—an Emerson on one side, a Hawthorne on the other.

Small wonder, then, that nightmare lurks on the other side of the American dream, or that when one utopian project after another comes to ruin, it reestablishes itself over the next hill and with a new name. As Hofstadter's article demonstrates, incarnations of the paranoid style surfaced as early as 1798, when Jedidiah Morse warned his congregants that "secret and systematic means have been adopted and pursued . . . to undermine the foundations of this Religion, and to overthrow its Altars." But I suspect that a more thorough search of Puritan sermons would have revealed that Morse was hardly the first minister to worry about conspiratorial forces out to undermine communal welfare. Indeed, Bradford's *Of Plymouth Planation* (1630-51) is a tale of Paradise founded, developed, and lost. In Bradford's words "some kind of wickedness did grow and break forth there, in a land where the same was so much witness and so narrowly looked into." Granted, Bradford did not fulminate about "secret and systematic means"—in this case, the enemy was nothing more, nor less, than private property and the enormous opportunities the New World presented "for the enriching of themselves"—that so weakened his church, but neither did he skimp on assigning the blame to what might be called the American condition. The City of God was best thought and talked about on board ships such as the *Arabella* (site of John Winthrop's "A Model of Christian Charity") than on the land Pilgrims discovered when they disembarked.

My point is not that America has a monopoly on manifestations of the paranoid style, but rather that the expectations which formed our national character can produce more than a fair share of conspiratorial drumbeating. Again, Hofstadter's tissue of quotations—separated by 50 years and extending in a seamless pattern from Jedidiah Morse to Joseph McCarthy—suggests that intimations of the apocalypse can always be counted on to pack the house. But here is where Hofstadter and I part company, for I would argue that the years since President Kennedy's assassination have significantly altered the general public's perception of what "conspiracies" are and of how widespread they might be. Much of Hofstadter's surveying effort netted such fish as the anti-Masonic agitation, those alarmed by the implications of Mormonism, and Populist writers who railed against international bankers. Nativists and Know-Nothings, it would seem, have always been with us; but there is a mighty difference between the internecine religious squabbles buried in our past and the deep distrust of government that is our present condition. In short, any contemporary conspiracy theory worth its salt finds its targets no lower than the highest levels.

Granted, the slave-holding South did not hesitate to blame Lincoln for its woes, nor did the Far Right hesitate to take a Roosevelt—and later even an Eisenhower—to task for weakening America's moral fiber. Still, in the years since the Kennedy assassination, not only has public distrust deepened, but more important, it has moved inexorably from the fringes to the mainstream.

III

At this point let me focus on three large cultural convulsions and suggest how they have become inextricably entangled with the American imagination. I begin with the *Kulturkampf* that raged during the 1930s and 40s, and that sharply divided

Stalinists from anti-Stalinists, anti-Communists from anti-anti-Communists, true believers from maverick radicals. Given recent events, many of the defining moments of earlier times, other places—everything from rallies to whip up sympathy for the Rosenbergs to orchestrated, pro-Soviet ventures such as the 1949 Waldorf World Peace Conference—must now seem of interest only to those plugging away on doctoral dissertations. Nor need one resort to a door-stopping tome such as Allan Wald's *The New York Intellectuals* (1987) to realize that the impetus behind much of the polemical firepower often boiled down to these questions: was Stalinism, with its ugly purges and totalitarian excess, an aberration, or was it the logical, even predictable, result of ideas that could no longer be believed, much less served? Could one remain committed to the Russian Revolution by blaming Stalin alone for the crimes that had been perpetrated in the Revolution's name, or was it possible that a genuine workers' revolution had not yet occurred?

For those who manned the typewriters at intellectual magazines such as Philip Rahv's *Partisan Review* or Dwight Macdonald's *Politics*, such questions were hardly academic, nor were the polemics that resulted simply an occasion to show off brilliance. Rather, the anguish in the years before and after the Stalin-Hitler pact was part of a protracted struggle for the 20th-century's political soul. At least that is how many of the New York intellectuals saw their fight against all that the word "Stalinism" represented.

Beyond the Hudson, of course, things were a good deal simpler. Anyone caught standing under a Marxist umbrella and throwing around terms like "dialectics" or "historical necessity" was *a priori* a suspicious, anti-American sort. Xenophobia explains the general animus that produced the Immigration and Nationality (McCarran-Walter) Act of 1952 and energized the likes of Senator Theodore G. Bilbo, Congressman John R. Rankin, and Gerald L. K. Smith; anti-Semitism accounts for the particulars. As conspiracy theories go, the line about "international bankers" and "warmongering international Jewry" has had a long, shameful run in American history. And at least since the days of Henry Ford, the old lies perpetrated in the *Protocols of the Elders of Zion* have been trotted out by one demagogue after another. As Rankin put it, in sentiments widely shared by the Far Religious Right: American Jews are "[t]he same gang that composed the Fifth Column of the Crucifixion, [that] hounded the Savior during the days of his ministry, [and] persecuted him to his ignominious death . . . For nearly two millennia Jews have overrun and virtually destroyed Europe. Now they are trying to undermine and destroy America." Hofstadter could not have hoped for a better, more pointed illustration of the paranoid style as it reared its head in American politics.

Nonetheless, the more theoretically inclined on the Far Left continued to operate on the assumption that what the age required was yet another ponderous recitation on capitalism's collective failure. Others knew better. Cultural warfare requires that one tilt the playing field of culture itself—by holding better parties, writing better songs, and perhaps most of all, putting one's faith in the imagination rather than the disembodied intellect. Whatever the shortcomings of the radical Left, however much internecine squabbles depleted ranks or turned firepower inward, it knew how to generate sympathy for "official" martyrs like the Rosenbergs. And as novels such as E. L. Doctorow's *The Book of Daniel* (1971) or Robert Coover's *The Public Burning* (1977) make clear, what keeps the fires of true belief blazing is the conviction that conspiracy's invisible hand has been at work in the highest reaches of government. Moreover, once the "new journalism" so blurred the line between fiction and fact that writers no longer had to worry about creating the imaginative plausibility of the former or adhere to the normal responsibilities associated with the latter, anything—absolutely *anything*—seemed fair game. So, despite the mounting evidence that Julius Rosenberg was probably guilty (and Ethel probably was not), Doctorow's exercise in nostalgia on the left creates a thinly veiled *roman à clef* that only apologists of the first water could believe, and only the politically naïve could accept at face value.

If it is true that time blurs the outlines of history—and I would argue that this is doubly true in a land where ahistoricity has been the norm, and where mythologies weigh more heavily than fact—it is also true that time is the unwitting ally of those artists with highly selective (and often, self-serving) memories. One thinks, for example, if Lillian Hellman and the ways she systematically went about creating not only a "Julia" such as never was, but also a rendition of the McCarthy years that gives the term "whitewash" whole new meanings: "Most of the Communists I had met [Ms. Hellman argues] seemed to me people who wanted to make a better world; many of them were silly people and a few of them were genuine nuts, but that doesn't make for denunciations." Not so, Irving Howe replied in thunder, and in ways that simultaneously set the record straight and in the process, put the self-mythologizing Ms. Hellman in her place:

> Most of the Communists Miss Hellman met may have wanted a better world, but the better world they wanted came down to a soul-destroying and body-torturing prison: the Moscow trials, the Stalin dictatorship, the destruction of millions during the forced collectivization, and a systematic denial of the slave camps in Siberia. . . . Those who supported Stalinism and its political enterprises, either here or abroad, helped befoul the cultural atmosphere, helped bring totalitarian methods into trade unions, helped perpetuate one of the great lies of our century, helped destroy whatever possibilities there might have been for a resurgence of serious radicalism. Isn't that harm enough?

Granted, a writer such as Coover does not have the same apologist agenda. No doubt *The Public Burning* was intended to hold Nixon's feet to the satiric fire; and given the sad debacle of Watergate, who can say that his instincts were wrong. But genuine satire is made of sterner, more disciplined stuff than the high jinks overpraised as postmodernism. Nor is Outrage alone sufficient—not for *The Public Burning*, and certainly not for Philip Roth's sophomoric effort at Nixon-bashing called *Our Gang* (1971).

Meanwhile, something of the old, dangerously romantic beat goes on among those academicians who find themselves drawn to the victimized, persecuted, and oppressed—and who insist that conspiracies explain the cultural landscape in ways that *Realpolitik* cannot. I am confident that one could trudge across each of the newly formed federated Soviet states without bumping into a single Marxist critic (at least one eager to engage in dialectical banter), but I can turn up at least three doctrinaire Marxists by simply strolling over to my college's department of economics. I'm told that larger colleges are even luckier, and that our most prestigious universities are packed with folks who make a good buck in "oppression studies." I take a measure of comfort in this, because one sure way to know if an idea is inert is to ask if somebody can get tenure by perpetuating it. Apparently, Marxism and its cousin neo- have met the test and are doing quite nicely, thank you.

In the old days of *Kulturkampf*—when cultural warfare

still retained a more than passing acquaintance with the reality principle and when the stark evidence before one's eyes counted for something—people modified their positions, adjusted their verbal fire, even "broke ranks." As such, the Stalin-Hitler pact became an occasion for anguished soul-searching about a Marxist god that had clearly failed; and later, the uglier aspects of the New Left caused many to forge new alliances during the 1970s. Now one can become what Hofstadter would have reckoned impossible—namely, a guerrilla with tenure.

In this sense, Hofstadter's thesis, restricted as it was to the machinations of the Far Right, tells only a partial tale. The bald truth is that, during the decades between, say, 1935 and 1955, there was bad faith and deep suspicion on both ends of the political spectrum, as those who worried about Commies under their bed were matched by those equally worried that *any* criticism directed at Moscow was tantamount to fascism. But the fringes were precisely that—extremes meriting attention, as, say, Joseph McCarthy merited attention—but that did not speak to the mainstream.

Those unwilling to give up their fascinations with the "evil empire" of communism are of course still with us, even if communism *per se* is not. After all, nothing quite explains our collective mess—the agitation for gay and lesbian rights, the abortion rights movement, or federally funded pornographic art—like communism. To imagine other possibilities is, in effect, to deny a life's work devoted to standing four-square against the devil incarnate. So, those who once linked flying saucers and assorted UFO's with communism on an extraterrestrial scale or who equate the mass media with left-liberal indoctrination see continuing evidence of the old plots. But that said, how is this very different from those with an equally compelling psychological need to believe that the Rosenbergs were framed or that every Red scare (and every Red) was, at bottom, a right-wing fabrication? The former produces copy for supermarket tabloids such as the *National Enquirer*; the latter, leaden ideology between hard covers.

IV

Meanwhile, newer, shinier conspiracy theories have rolled off the assembly line. Young urban blacks, for example, have been especially susceptible to those who can spin out facile plots with the reckless abandon and imaginative daring that once went into "playing the dozens." Nothing, it seems, is too far-fetched, too outlandish, to get a hearing—be it Chicago politician Gus Savage's claim that AIDS was invented by Jewish doctors bent on black genocide, or Professor Leonard Jeffries' much-publicized division of the known world into "sun people" and their icy counterparts. But however much the individual plots may differ, what they have in common is a belief that black troubles are the result of conspiracies hatched "out there"—by the white world in general and Jews in particular.

Small wonder, then, that Malcolm X has been rediscovered by a generation proud to wear an X baseball cap or a T-shirt with Malcolm brandishing a firearm over the words "by all means necessary." As Spike Lee's *Do the Right Thing* stridently insists, Martin Luther King, Jr. pales when compared to Malcolm X in much the same way that "We Shall Overcome" is no match for Public Enemy's "Fight the Power." In much the same self-styled arithmetic, Alex Haley's *Roots* has taken a back seat to the more memorable, in-your-face sections he recorded in *The Autobiography of Malcolm X.* Given these realities—and the realization that militant posturing is a special prerogative of the young—what can one who happens to be white and of a certain age say? That *The Autobiography of Malcolm X* is a tale of *several* Malcolms, not only the one who railed against the "white devil" and the sham of integration, but also the one who came to embrace much deeper, more compassionate, more genuinely religious visions in the months before his assassination; or that black history is filled with personalities (one thinks of W. E. B. DuBois, of Richard Wright) who were every bit as complicated, evolving, and important as Malcolm X? Unfortunately, the *Zeitgeist* seems in no mood for such instruction. Conspiracy-hawkers are in the saddle, and they ride us, blacks as well as whites.

Consider the current ballyhoo about Afrocentrism. Would that it serve to swell the enrollment of black students in classics departments or, better yet, inspire them to pursue careers in the sciences. But the sad truth is that while studies such as Martin Bernal's *Black Athena* have sparked serious debate about what we know, and do not know, about classical antiquity, their dubious claim to fame is that they convince those who know little Sanskrit and less Greek that Eurocentrism itself is a lie, and

Western culture essentially a theft. Indeed, in the hands of charlatans like Professor Jeffries, Afrocentrism quickly degenerates into demagogery. No doubt his unabashed opportunism must strike serious black scholars as an embarrassment, in much the same way that I used to wince whenever pundits floated the idea of Meir Kahane as a "spokeman" for the Jewish people. The difference, however—and it is a crucial one—is that the mainstream Jewish community did everything it could to distance itself from a dangerous bigot like Kahane and to disabuse the general public about his clout. By contrast, most black scholars have been conspicuous by their public silence.

Perhaps the black scholars who built their careers on book after book are no better positioned to derail a conspiracy of such gargantuan proportions than I am. Indeed, they might well argue that black intellectuals lack the popular support of a charismatic, highly theatrical type like Professor Jeffries; but, if that is so, they should not feign surprise when African-American studies programs are dismantled in the next decades. For surely the claim that European culture is a lie is itself a lie that has no place among those devoted to pursuing the truth. But that said, how could one *prove* that the loopier claims of Afrocentrists are so much rot—especially when their claim rests on a belief that the glories of African culture have been systematically falsified or willfully erased. For the hide-bound conspiracy theorist, the very absence of proof *is* proof, yet another instance (should more be needed) of the insidious workings of one's enemy. This, of course, is the paranoid style operating at its deepest level, and, given our deteriorating racial situation, one is hardly surprised to find Professor Jeffries' pronouncements splattered across the pages of *The New York Times*. If he had not come along he would have been invented—no doubt by a novelist in the Tom Wolfe, *Bonfire of the Vanities* mold.

V

Which brings me, at long last, to the "mother" of contemporary conspiracy theory—the Kennedy assassination. If Shakespeare is, as Joyce puts it in *Ulysses*, "the happy hunting-ground of minds that have lost their balance" and if Joyce himself became the modern equivalent for generations of dedicated, nitpicking Joyceans, what is one to say of the 600+ articles and books devoted to proving that Kennedy was gunned down by (a) the CIA, (b) the Mafia, (c) the Far Right, (d) the Far Left, or (e) all of the above? Those of us who lived through the immediate aftermath of that shattering event remember where we were and what we were doing with a precision not likely to be matched by any other single moment; and I suspect I am not alone in feeling that our world had been altered in the split second it took the bullets to make their way from the Texas School Book Depository to President Kennedy's head. The fifties and all they signified—everything from innocence to the certainty of certainty—exploded, and we are still trying to awake from the nightmare that the history of Nov. 22, 1963 created.

Indeed, as other assassinations followed—first Malcolm X, then Martin Luther King, Jr., and finally Bobby Kennedy—the words "We interrupt this broadcast for a special news bulletin" took on an ominous cast, one that has not completely disappeared from my consciousness or my viscera. As the decades passed, however, I began to realize that the date of Kennedy's assassination had metamorphosed itself into an exam question which meant, of course, that a certain percentage of high school students would get it wrong,—initially by one or two years, then five, until it finally settled comfortably into that all-purpose guess for everything from the completion of the Panama Canal to the gunfight at the OK corral: 1885. The sheer popularity of Oliver Stone's *JFK* may change all that, although the cynical part of me suspects that students are more likely to remember when they saw the film than when Kennedy was assassinated.

More important, my earlier quarrels with novels that conflate history and fiction redouble when the issue turns on docudramas such as *JFK*. For whatever else Stone might be, he is a man with an agenda that goes well beyond the entertainment value of a well-made film. He not only means to raise questions about a wide-spread coverup, but also to tie the whole unseemly package to the war in Vietnam. As Stone would have it, a Kennedy on the verge of pulling our troops out of Vietnam was a Kennedy who had effectively signed his death warrant. The CIA was only too happy to oblige, and to pin the rap on a certifiable patsie like Oswald in the bargain.

That film packs a wallop print seldom matches is true enough; but when one so cleverly intersperses documentary footage with simulated action that audiences accept as real—especially for those who think a Zapruder is a German sports car—the net effect quickly becomes an exercise in manipulation. *JFK* means to sow doubt, and even Stone's sharpest critics would admit that this is a case of "Mission Accomplished." If the political primaries have taught us anything, it is that Americans are fed up and not about to take it anymore. It's a dangerous recipe that makes for such unlikely candidates as Pat Buchanan or H. Ross Perot; and for political wannabes like Stone.

Curiously enough, Oliver Stone may be the most insidious of the bunch—not only because he knows how to project himself as Ron Kovic, the disillusioned Vietnam vet or Jim Garrison, the New Orleans attorney on a mission from God, but also because, at bottom, he sees himself as a Frank Capra for the 1990s. The difference, of course, is that *his* Mr. Deeds is—indeed, *must be*—broken on the conspiratorial wheel. What Stone gives us is, in his words, an "alternate history," one at once truer to the facts than the account served up by the Warren Commission and "truer" in terms of the deeper rhythms of myth. For Stone, an event as decisive, as disturbing, as the murder of a President must have causations co-equal to the effect. A lone, crazed Oswald simply won't do in much the same way that the "single ['magic'] bullet" theory won't wash.

Conspiracy theorists suggested much the same thing as the nation mourned the death of Lincoln. John Wilkes Booth simply couldn't have worked his way to Lincoln's box at the Ford Theatre without a network of fellow conspirators and those in the shadows holding the pursestrings. But much as we yearn for bona fide martyrs (both as explanation and consolation), modern life is not Greek tragedy any more than the Kennedy years were Camelot. Moreover, even if Stone *et al.* get their fondest wish—namely, that every document, every scrap of paper, currently under wraps be released to public scrutiny—I suspect that nothing would convince them that essential documents had not been altered or systematically destroyed. At a March 3, 1992 Town Hall Meeting sponsored by *Nation* magazine, Norman Mailer argued that our Hobson's choice with respect to the Kennedy assassination was apathy or paranoia. I would respectfully submit that common sense and a healthy regard for what we *do* know about Nov. 22, 1963 suggest another possibility—namely, that the Warren Commission's conclusion was, in large measure, correct.

Granted, things as they are (or seem) are *changed* when played on what Wallace Stevens called "a blue guitar." The imagination seeks a Truth deeper than truth, a Reality more patterned, more coherent, than the messy affair that brought a president and an Oswald to Dealey Plaza. But what if one's imaginative musings turn naturally to conspiratorial visions? I am thinking, of course, about Don DeLillo and the fact that in his novels the world "plot" is more likely to be a dark pun on conspiracy than a description of "what happens next." As one character in *Running Dog* (1978) puts it: "This is the age of conspiracy." Indeed, visions of conspiracy dance through the eleven novels DeLillo has published since 1971; and given the sheer range of his subjects—football players, rock stars, mad scientists, television executives, college professors, professional terrorists—one can only conclude that what these disparate characters share is DeLillo's insistence that "all conspiracies are the same taut story of men who find coherence in some criminal act."

In this sense, *Libra* (1988), DeLillo's contribution to our national obsession with Kennedy's assassination, was a natural. He could not only put an imaginative spin on Lee Harvey Oswald, his mother, Marguerite, and Jack Ruby, but also add as many anti-Castro Cuban exiles, CIA operatives, and Mafia wheeler-dealers as the baggy traffic of a novel would bear. Better yet, speeches like the following seem to come with the imaginative territory, however much they smack of pure DeLillo rather than the cynical CIA agent who actually utters them: "The dangerous secrets used to be held outside the government. Plots, conspiracies, secrets of revolution, secrets of the social order. Now it's government that has a lock on the secrets that matter. All the danger is in the White House, from nuclear weapons on down." Those who raced in to disagree (America might be less than perfect, but it certainly wasn't *this* bad) were met by rolling eyeballs and the all-purpose retort of the late 1980s: "You just don't get it, do you? . . . You just don't get it."

As I write these lines, the first wave of mainstream journalism is taking the measure of Susan Faludi's *Backlash*, a book out to argue that the gains of the Women's Movement were systematically undermined during the Reagan years—by "a kind of pop-culture version of the Big Lie" perpetrated by the Religious Right, the fashion industry, and perhaps most of all, popular films such as *Fatal Attraction*. At times Faludi seems to back off from calling the equation that "freedom equals unhappiness" a full-blown conspiracy, but it is hard to turn her 550 pages without feeling that feminists have been *had*. Indeed, her forays into history suggest that *Backlash* owes as large a debt to Richard Hofstadter as to Betty Freidan. I intend to stay tuned as the feminists slug it out in much the same way that I figure we have not heard the last from those tonguing a sore tooth about the Kennedy assassination. At the Town Hall meeting I mentioned earlier, Mailer also suggested that it might be interesting to speculate about the timing of the Watergate scandal, given Nixon's movement toward détente. After all, if the Right feared that Kennedy would yank us out of Vietnam, the Right might also have been skittish about a Nixon playing footsie with the commies. Even Stone perked up at that one. After all, Hollywood directors feed on controversy every bit as much as media hounds; and at the moment nothing plays better in Dubuque than products of America's conspiratorial imagination. Moreover, as Hofstadter knew full well, they always did.

Irving Howe's Negro Problem—and Ours

> What, then, was the experience of a man with a black skin, what *could* it be in this country? How could a Negro put pen to paper, how could he so much as think or breathe, without some impulsion to protest, be it harsh or mild, political or private, released or buried.
>
> —from Irving Howe's "Black Boys and Native Sons"

With the possible exception of Lionel Trilling, no New York Jewish intellectual wrote paragraphs that rang with greater authority, indeed, a larger magisterial presence, than did Irving Howe's; and yet having made the claim, one hastens to add that the "magisterial," both as temperament and defining style, expressed itself quite differently in the two men. For Trilling, the M-word was often synonymous with other M-words such as Mandarin and mannered, while, for Howe, it was generally associated with moral, and more particularly with a moral politics unafraid to utter its true name: socialism. Given these distinctions, it is hardly surprising that Trilling felt no special attraction to black writers or that Howe did, for the complicated sociocultural strands that, taken together, comprised what Trilling called the "liberal imagination" were noticeably absent in the rawer experiences black writers recounted.

By contrast, these experiences were precisely what prompted Howe to write "Black Boys and Native Sons," and then to defend his assumptions about how black writers ought properly to respond to social injustice in a series of exchanges with a young, intellectually feisty novelist named Ralph Ellison—and then, with few exceptions, to maintain a stony, stoical silence about blacks that lasted until his death.

Hence, "Irving Howe's Negro Problem—and Ours," a title

shamelessly adapted from Norman Podhoretz's "My Negro Problem—and Ours" (*Commentary*, 1963), and meant to suggest a way of testing squabbles from the recent past against our current troubles. That a later section of my argument will focus directly on Podhoretz's essay may help to soften those of a mind to charge me with an unduly appropriated title; but I also suspect that such folks will have lots more to fret about in the pages that follow. For title aside, what my thesis intends to explore is a case for demystification and dialogue at a cultural moment when versions of separatism appear to be in the saddle.

The Howe-Ellison debate—now largely forgotten by all but cultural historians—represents disagreement at a level of intelligence and sheer eloquence that is sorely missed, and I would add, much needed. For by bringing the competing claims of Art and Life into sharp relief—and in the process, tempering Ellison's hopes for a literature simultaneously black and American against Howe's insistence that art be forged with a full consciousness of one's political responsibilities and fate—one sees the central problem of our time in bold relief.

In this regard, let me begin with a curious paragraph plucked from a recent issue of *Partisan Review* devoted to political correctness. It was written by Mark Mirsky, a writer who teaches at City College, and details a conversation (or perhaps more accurately, a non-conversation) he had with Irving Howe about Leonard Jeffries:

> No one on the campus easily discusses Professor Jeffries, because we are most of us, as my former student and colleague Michelle Walker, has pointed out, intimidated. "Just knowing he's down the hall makes discussion of race and ethnicity loaded," she told an interviewer for *The New Yorker*. We have all seen the professor walking down the corridors with what seems to be a praetorian guard, and some of us wonder why this is happening on an academic campus. We read in the *Harvard Crimson* interview what threats were made to the interviewee and shuddered. . . . I was quite shocked however when the late Irving Howe, once my professor, expressed outrage at the Levin case, but fell into a deep swoon of silence when I tried to press him on that of Professor Jeffries, Chairman of the African American Studies Department.

Like many others, I have been following the respective cases of Professors Levin and Jeffries from the sidelines, relying on the *New York Times* to reflect accurately who said what, where, when, and why. Mirsky, by contrast, has an insider's feel for a Zeitgeist I get only at second-hand. Nonetheless, I read his words with shock and not a little skepticism, for the portrait of Howe he paints does not square with the man I knew, and who insisted that I call him "Irving." Indeed, of all the accusations hurled his way during a long, often stormy career, silence—much less moral silence—was never one of them. His double-whammy of intelligence and passion could be intimidating, and his gruff manner was hardly designed to put antagonists at ease. Still, even if one readily acknowledges that the last decades often catapulted him into deep depression (he worried about much that struck him as coarsening cultural debate), I find it hard to imagine that he would be rendered quipless, even if he felt that Jeffries was a clown or that Mirsky was a boor.

The result is yet another occasion (as if more were needed) that confirms the truth of Auden's lines on the death of Yeats—namely, that "The words of the dead are [or at least, *are likely to be*] modified in the guts of the living." Let me also confess that long after a thick issue's worth of arguments mounted up against the chilling effects of "political correctness" had blurred, what I couldn't get out of my head was the image of an Irving Howe unwilling, or unable, to go on record—even if the "record" were one of casual conversation with an obviously (and rightly) agitated writer—about a racist demagogue like Jeffries. Coming to terms with that specter is finally what this essay is about, even when it may seem to be making side excursions by way of large cultural loops.

Since *Partisan Review*'s most recent symposium was the setting for Mirsky's comment, and because Irving has a long association with that journal's pages, let me use the connection as a way of gazing backward and, eventually, of bringing his time line, and ours, to the present moment. Those who remember the *Partisan Review*'s heyday will no doubt recall earlier symposia issues such as "Our Country and Its Culture" (1951-52) and the ways that the gathering between its covers helped to sharpen the debate about an intellectual postwar attitude and agenda. Granted, there were polemical disagreements in print and not a few longstanding friendships broke up over private conversations (Given the testy *Partisan Review* crowd, was there really any other possibility?), but one had the feeling that, once the intellectual dust had settled, a rough consensus would have been reached. I stress the word *rough* because maverick intellectuals work on the assumption that if an idea is too widely shared, there must be something wrong with it; and true to form, when talk about the end of the old adversary culture was joined with talk about the birth of a new alliance between postwar affluence and intellectual influence (read: respectability), Howe and Norman Mailer wrote down their sense of the appalling result in a single word: conformity.

My hunch is that Howe probably agreed with the general assessment of Trilling as Columbia's "court Jew," but I can also remember him telling me, with great fondness, about occasions when he and Trilling met to talk about the nuances that layer themselves around a slippery term like "vulgar." Still, no matter how eloquently Diana Trilling's recent memoir pleads its case for a self-doubting, conflicted, and altogether "blocked" Trilling, it was the overly cultivated, even precious Ivy League professor who must have made the more plebian Howe bristle. And while Howe kept much of this to himself (unlike, say, the Alfred Kazin who makes a point of settling Trilling's imperious hash in his in-your-face autobiography, *New York Jew*), everything about their lives suggests that the residue of an immigrant Jewish childhood defined aspects of Howe in ways that it never did for Trilling.

Intellectual disagreements were, however, quite another matter, and in "This Age of Conformity" (1954), Howe made it abundantly clear that he did not share Trilling's optimism about a cultural moment he [Trilling] defined as the point "where wealth shows a tendency to submit itself, in some degree, to the rule of mind and imagination, to apologize for its existence by a show of taste and sensitivity." For Howe, it was not "wealth" or for that matter the ideology of capitalism that was doing the submitting, but, rather, intellectuals themselves. They—and in particular, Trilling—were not only deluded, but also dangerous.

And so it was that *Dissent*, the journal Howe and Mailer brought into being shortly after they found themselves on the short end of the *Partisan Review* "consensus," came into being. One result bears directly on the topic at hand—namely, the publication of Mailer's "The White Negro" (1957) in *Dissent*'s pages. In its day, the essay was regarded as seminal stuff, reading absolutely required if one were to get a handle on the main lever of contemporary culture. But as Irving explained (confessed?) in a telling footnote to his 1969 essay, "The New York Intellectuals," he "bears a heavy responsibility for publishing the essay and should have stated "his objections to the passage in which Mailer discusses the morality of beating up a fifty-year-old storekeeper." I would only add that, troubling as Mailer's celebration of violence surely is, the outlandish equation of its title is at least equally disturbing. For however it might be gussied up with flashy turns of phrase or the patina of social criticism masquerading as philosophy, what the essay insists upon is a dangerously romantic construction that mystifies black folk at the same time that it reduced them to stereotype.

One could argue, of course, that however much Mailer may have hoped that his essay would call the "white Negro" into being, only intellectuals—or in my circle, graduate students aspiring to become intellectual players—took his ponderous remarks seriously. What mattered more centrally were the first calls to Black Power and then the successive waves of separatist ideology. These versions of militance had a romantic appeal, one pitched to people fully prepared to act on their premises rather than to chat about them over cups of cappuccino. Indeed, as the differences that separated Old and New Left became apparent (and perhaps tragically unavoidable), Irving stayed the course with those blacks who struck him as committed, effective agents for social change. Of these, none was more important to him than Bayard Rustin, a man he admired greatly, and whom he counted among his important models.

By contrast, Irving's 1965 essay, "New Styles in 'Leftism,'" made it clear that he saw little to admire among those longer on flamboyant style than substance, and this including the emerging black nationalists he regarded as problematic and deeply disturbing. Yet, even here, he offered up his analysis with large doses of respect for a figure like Malcolm X, but also with a sense that there was not a sufficient understanding of how politics worked for his message to stand even the slimmest chance of success. A difficult juggling act? Certainly, and one that earned Howe's candor as much derision as had greeted Podhoretz's. Let me quote the relevant paragraph, partly in an effort to set the historical record straight, and partly as a way of suggesting that our tortured racial history seems destined to reduplicate itself with the slimmest margin of difference:

> *Black Nationalism.* Here is a creed that speaks or appears to speak totally against compromise, against negotiating with "the white power structure," against the falsities of white liberals, indeed, against anything but an indulgence of verbal violence. Shortly be-

> fore his tragic death, Malcolm X spoke at a Trotskyist-sponsored meeting and listening to him I felt, as did others, that he was in a state of internal struggle, reaching out for an ideology he did not yet have. For the Negroes in his audience he offered the relief of articulating subterranean feelings of hatred, contempt, defiance, feelings that did not have to be held in check because there was a tacit compact that the talk about violence would remain talk. For both the Negroes and whites in the audience there was an apparent feeling that Malcolm and Malcolm alone among the Negro spokesmen was authentic because . . . well, because finally he spoke for nothing but his rage, for no proposal, no plan, no program, just a sheer outpouring of anger and pain. And that they could understand. The formidable sterility of his speech, so impressive in its relation to a deep personal suffering, touched something in their hearts. For Malcolm, intransigent in words and nihilistic in reality, never invoked the possibility or temptations of immediate struggles; he never posed the problems, confusions, and risks of maneuver, compromise, retreat. Brilliantly Malcolm spoke for a rejection so complete it transformed him into an apolitical spectator, or in the language of his admirers, a "cop-out."

Granted, Irving wrote these words at a time when he must have felt acutely lonely, when the new wave of activists must have struck him not only as narcissistic and indulgent, but also as thoroughly unschooled in the rigor and discipline that leftist politics requires.

Meanwhile, he continued to use the pages of *Dissent* in an effort to provide clarity and vision to the national debate about race, and in the process to bring younger black intellectuals such as Cornel West into the fold; indeed, at a time when many emerging black academics bemoaned the fact that they were effectively frozen out of mainstream intellectual journals. *Dissent* had a better track record than most. To be sure, West's commitment to democratic socialism had something to do with Howe's generosity (I suspect that he was a good deal less impressed by the prophetic evangelicalism West espoused), but what matters, finally, is that Howe found a contemporary black voice he could respect without reservation or contretemps.

All of which returns me to my original quandry about what looks for all the world like two very different Irvings—the one who made no bones about the accommodationist direction *Partisan Review* seemed to be taking in 1952, and the one who apparently could not muster up enough moral courage to take on a laughably easy target such as Jeffries. I begin with a simple, but crucially important term: selection. Unless a critic means to address *everything* making a claim on behalf of culture, he or she must choose the battles worth the sweat writing requires. Or as the Yiddish maxim would have it, "A fool can toss a stone into a lake where even six sages cannot find it."

Part of Howe's authority derives from his Olympian view of the culturally important, and his insistence that the writers who mattered most were "witnesses" to the great struggles of our time. Thus, in roughly the same way that poems write poets (rather than the other way around), Howe's best criticism depended at least as much on his social passion and political engagement as it did on his acumen as a reader of subtle literary textures. The result was an internal dialectic, one that could readily admit that, on strictly aesthetic grounds, writers such as Ignatzio Silone or Arthur Koestler may not weather the stiffer tests of time, and still insist that what made their works valuable, even essential, was a value that transcended the niceties of New Critical standards. As Howe put it in *A Margin of Hope*, their questions "were also mine."

Enter Richard Wright, and the beginnings of what I am calling Howe's "Negro problem." For what he saw in *Native Son* was a confirmation of everything he associated with long-standing social injustice and the necessity of artistic protest:

> The day *Native Son* appeared, American culture was changed forever. No matter how much qualifying the book might later need, it made impossible a repetition of the old lies. In all its crudeness, melodrama, and claustrophobia of vision, Richard Wright's novel brought out into the open, as one never had before, the hatred, fear, and violence that have crippled and may yet destroy our culture. . . . A blow at the white man, the novel forced him to recognize himself as an oppressor. A blow at the black man, the novel forced him to recognize the cost of his submission.

Native Son was, in short, *the* Negro novel that successive generations of black writers, understandably enough, would struggle against, but never quite supplant, for it had put an awkward finger on the only problem worth writing about in the first place. The very best that "black boys" like James Baldwin and Ralph Ellison could hope to achieve is a bit of space as Oedipal sons out to pull down their father. Meanwhile, the image of Bigger Thomas remained, forever stuck into the heads of its readers, black and white alike:

> Brutal and brutalized, lost forever to his unexpended hatred and his fear of the world, a numbed and illiterate black boy stumbling into a murder and never, not even at the edge of the electric chair, breaking through to an understanding of either his plight or himself, Bigger Thomas was a part of Richard Wright, a part even of James Baldwin who stared with horror at Wright's Bigger, unable either to absorb him into his consciousness or reject him from it. Enormous courage, a discipline of self-conquest, was required to conceive Bigger Thomas, for this was no eloquent Negro spokesman, no admirable intellectual or formidable proletarian. Bigger was drawn—one would surmise, deliberately—from white fantasy and white contempt. Bigger was the worst of Negro life accepted, then rendered a trifle conscious and thrown back at those who made him what he was. "No American Negro exists," Baldwin would later write, "who does not have his private Bigger Thomas living in his skull."

Let us admit that Howe has rightly assessed the raw power Wright's portrait of Bigger Thomas continues to exert while also admitting that Howe's formulation sells the black experience and, more important the black imagination, far too short. For if Bigger Thomas is simultaneously product and prophet of an America doomed to destruction, there is little to be done and even less to be said. The choice, as Howe's unflinching swoon seems to suggest, is between a darkness that descends on the unknowing and one that falls on those whose eyes have been skimmed by Wright's words.

Small wonder that Baldwin and Ellison bristled under the lash of Howe's johnny-one-note criticism and the sting of his dismissal. For in arguing against the severe limitations of the "protest" novel Baldwin meant to loosen the ties that would forever bind blacks to the categorizations of social victim and mythic sexual animal. Was there not, he kept asking in early essays such as "Everybody's Protest Novel" and "Many Thousands Gone," a richer, more artistically expansive way of transcending the narrow confines of naturalist fiction? Howe, of course, had included Baldwin's arguments in his own essay, if only to dismiss them as yet another instance in the sad history of painful ruptures between younger writers and their now outdated models/mentors, and to confirm the subtler equations between sociology and literature that "black boys" like Baldwin fail to see: "If it is true, as Baldwin said in 'Everybody's Protest Novel,' that 'literature and sociology are not one and the same,' it is equally true that such statements hardly begin to cope with the problem of how a writer's own experience affects his desire to represent human affairs in a work of fiction." For Howe, Baldwin's formula was too easy by half, missing as it did everything that makes social experience an important—yea, a necessary ingredient—in compelling fiction. Howe, in short, was fully prepared to counter Baldwin's objections, and as the sad arc of Baldwin's career played itself out, he may even have experienced the cold consolation of feeling he had been right all along.

Ellison, however, was another matter, for his "The World and the Jug," an extended reply to "Black Boys and Native Sons," surely must have caught Irving off-guard and in an essentially untenable position. For Ellison argued that a view of black writing equating the authentic with the ferocious was both patronizing and deeply wrong-headed. Like the well-meaning friend who had once argued that Ellison "could not possibly write a novel because my experiences as a Negro had been too excruciating to allow me to achieve that psychological and emotional distance necessary for artistic creation," Howe apparently believed that "unrelieved suffering is the only 'real' Negro experience." Hence, the accusation that must have given Howe fits—namely, that "when he looks at a Negro he sees not a human being but an abstract embodiment of living hell"; and as a consequence, he utterly fails to see beyond the burden of blackness to the discipline those conditions inspire, and perhaps most important of all, to recognize the fullness, the richness, of black life "*despite* the realities of politics."

At this point, let me interject a few lines from Norman Podhoretz's "My Negro Problem—and Ours," an essay that certainly seemed more foolhardy than brave when it first appeared in 1963. Growing up in an integrated Brooklyn neighborhood, he had been told—and *in print* no less—two ideas that did not square with his experience: one, that all Jews were rich, and the other that all Negroes were persecuted. For a long time these cultural "truths" struck him as puzzlers because "the only Jews I knew were poor," and perhaps more important, that Negroes were doing the only persecuting I knew about, and, moreover, they were "doing it to *me*." The remaining lines of this paragraph were quite enough to brand Podhoretz, then and now, as a racist:

> A city boy's world is contained within three or four square blocks, and in my world it was the whites, the Italians and Jews, who feared the Negroes, not the

> other way around. The Negroes were tougher than we were, more ruthless, and on the whole they were better athletes. . . . Yet my sister's opinions, like print, were sacred, and when she told me about exploitation and economic forces I believed her. I believed her, but I was still afraid of Negroes. And I still hated them with all my heart.

Podhoretz would rightly insist that these were the feelings of a boy rather than the considered thoughts of an adult, but what his shameful, bitterly candid "confession" comes to is the shaping power of formative experience, and the considerable difference between Howe's memories and those of Podhoretz. For Irving, the largely Jewish immigrant milieu of the Depression Bronx hurt him into socialism. As he put it in the opening paragraphs of his intellectual autobiography, *A Margin of Hope*:

> The East Bronx, when I lived there as a boy, formed a thick tangle of streets crammed with Jewish immigrants from Eastern Europe, almost all of them poor. We lived in narrow five-story tenements, wall flush against wall, and with slate-colored stoops rising sharply in front. There never was enough space. . . . Hardly a day passed but someone was moving in or out. Often you could see a family's entire belongings—furniture, pots and pans, bedding, a tricycle—piled up on the sidewalks because they had been dispossessed.

By contrast, Podhoretz's world was shaped by rough-and-tumble Brooklyn, at a time before even Podhoretz's politically-correct sister knew the word, "multiculturalism." And while his accounts of black brutalization and white fear were decidedly *not* what America wanted to hear in 1963, some of his conclusions merit more than passing interest some thirty years later. For unlike many who rely on intellectual constructs alone, Podhoretz's ruminations on race have the virtue of being grounded in quotidian experience. He could, for example, understand the central point in Baldwin's early essays—namely, that Negroes hate the white man because he refuses to *look* at them—and add the following observation to a dialogue as deeply needed as it has been long delayed:

> What Baldwin does *not* tell us, however, is that the principle of facelessness is a two-way street and can operate in both directions with no difficulty at all. Thus, in my neighborhood in Brooklyn, *I* was as faceless to the Negroes as they were to me, and if they hated me because I never looked at them, I must also have hated them for never looking at *me*. To the Negroes, my white skin was enough to define me as the enemy, and

> in a war it is only the uniform that counts and not the person.

I suspect that much of the "confessional" strain in Podhoretz's essay must have struck Irving as overheated and inappropriate, which is perhaps only to say that he could be as reticent about the personal as he was often belligerent about the polemical. More important, I can imagine him wondering if anything meaningful, anything with a hint of justice or a smack of racial progress, is likely to come from this airing of one's "Negro problem"? I am guessing, of course, about what Irving might have felt in 1963, but there is little doubt that he was appalled by the tilt toward the neoconservative Right that the pages of *Commentary* magazine were taking under Podhoretz's heavy editorial hand.

What we "know," of course is that six years after Podhoretz's paragraphs effectively splintered the New York Jewish intellectuals into two camps—those eager to publicly distance themselves from such "racist" sentiments and those who silently whispered their agreement—Howe published "Black Boys and Native Sons." Although his initial impulse must have been to say a few kind words on behalf of Richard Wright at a time when younger black writers seemed bent on dismissing the abiding legacy of *Native Son,* Howe had clearly grabbed a hotter, more vexing wire than he had initially imagined. For what Ellison's "reply" comes to is nothing less than a contention that Howe not only missed the central point of his novel but also that he raced off (perhaps without being fully aware of the fact) to write an essay that adds yet another layer of "invisibility" to the long, serio-comic history recounted in *Invisible Man*'s pages.

Even more damning, Ellison made it clear that Howe must finally be counted with characters like Mr. Norton or Brother Jack because, like them, he is one who "would tell us the meaning of Negro life" without the bother of learning "how varied it really is." Not since Marx found himself shouting at London workers who gave the bum's rush to his complicated, interminable lectures about economics had there been such an icy stand-off between political theory and gritty, human reality; but this public squabble seemed far worse, partly because Ellison was an intellectual formed by the same books, nurtured by the same intellectual quarterlies, and committed to the same humane values as was Howe and partly because he beat Howe at his strong suit—namely, the literary essay.

Howe's reply—in the pages of *The New Leader*—probably gave his game away in a single sentence from his opening paragraph: "This is a mode of rebuttal that can soon become tiresome, but I would ask the reader to stick with me, for the outcome ought to be of general interest and not a mere personal defense." Unfortunately, what follows is instance upon instance of what only can be called "personal defense," for what Howe does is plead that he has been mightily misunderstood and that he meant merely to point out, in a manner neither unfriendly nor untruthful, that when a writer chooses not to participate directly in the Negro struggle and, instead, to "stick by his work as a novelist," that it is perhaps a costly decision to make.

Once again, Ellison's novel makes his own position as clear as we are likely to get—to wit, that even an invisible man, now fully, comically/tragically aware of his invisibility, has a "responsible social role to play." I have always read these words as a reflexive indicator that the novel we have just concluded is, in fact, that role, and that, as an artist, Ellison's responsibility is to tell stories as richly, as humanly, and most of all, as honestly as he can. Everything he has said—as well as what he has refused to say—in the years since confirms my original suspicions.

At the same time, however, Howe is surely right when he calls attention to the costs Ellison would likely bear for these decisions. And in truth, Ellison has had to suffer more abuse from blacks impatient with his uncompromising aesthetic position and jealous of his mainstream [read: Eurocentric] reputation than he ever had to endure from the likes of Irving Howe. If *Invisible Man* is included among the readings one might encounter in Black Studies programs—and, sadly, there are cases where instructors regard him as too old-fashioned, regressive, or politically incorrect to warrant inclusion—he is often offered up as a whipping boy, an "intellectual" too cozy with T. S. Eliot or James Joyce (to say nothing of the kind words he has heaved in the direction of Mark Twain or William Faulkner), to serve as other than a bad example.

Moreover, when Howe cobbled Baldwin and Ellison together as the "black boys" anxious to contend for Wright's mantle, Baldwin played a much larger part in the rebellious, Oedipal equation than did Ellison, no doubt because Baldwin clearly struck him as the greater writer. Nonetheless, it now seemed important for Howe to distinguish between his sense of plight and protest as "inseparable" from Negro experience and Ellison's wilfull misreading of plight-and-protest as *all*:

> Where serious discussion could begin, if Ellison troubled to represent my views with elementary good faith, would be in regard to the last of my quoted paragraphs. In what ways can a Negro writer—indeed any Negro—achieve "personal realization" as long as the American Negroes remain oppressed? To what extent can he achieve "personal realization" apart from the common effort of his people to win their full freedom? To what extent can he present a valid portrait of American Negro life without bringing in "plight and protest?"

One response, of course, might have been to ask Howe to reread *Invisible Man*, a novel that wonders, on one hand, if "politics can ever be an expression of love" and that demonstrates, on the other, how "personal realization" (a phrase the activist Howe clearly detests) can be best achieved through art. What Ellison's "Rejoinder"—also published in the pages of *The New Leader*—in fact did was make clear that he regarded himself as no less a custodian of the American language than Howe, and that above all else he considered himself an American writer. If Ellison had moments of self-doubt, it was not because he failed to measure up to Howe's—or others'—notion of political engagement, but rather because he failed to write as much as one who defined himself as a "writer" should.

While Howe remained stuck in metaphysical formulations of blackness, insisting, as so many others did, that because his heart was in the right place he could be as restrictive—and yes, as arbitrary—as he wished, Ellison insisted otherwise. Indeed, to all those who "publish interpretations of Negro experience which would not hold true for their own nor for any other form of life," Ellison felt an obligation to state the obvious—namely, that blacks were as various and surprising, as three dimensional, as human, and finally, as American as others; and that his view of what it meant to be a black writer simply did not square with Howe's reductive arithmetic:

> Howe makes of "Negroness" a metaphysical condition, one that is a state of irremediable agony which all but engulfs the mind. Happily, the view from inside the skin is not so dark as it appears to be from Howe's remote position, and therefore my view of "Negroness" is neither his nor that of the exponents of *negritude*. It is not skin color which makes a Negro American but cultural heritage as shaped by the American experience, the social and political predicament; a

> sharing of that "concord of sensibilities" which the group expresses through historical circumstance and through which it has come to constitute a sub-division of the larger American culture.

There, with Ellison's 1964 words, the case officially rested. Sadly, it has not been republished, and, indeed, one could argue that whatever differences separated them at the time have been overwhelmed by what Howe, in a 1969 postscript to "Black Boys and Native Sons," calls "an uncritical—which is, I think, patronizing acceptance—of Black Power ideology" that "would dismiss both Ellison and me as old-fashioned, irrelevant, and—most shattering of blows!—'mere liberal' advocates of 'integration.'" No doubt Howe chafed when Ellison set about instructing him in the range and depth of black experience (Howe, after all, was always more comfortable on the "giving" end of lectures, and he must have been driven to apoplexy when Black Power ideologues made it abundantly clear that Whitey's words were no longer welcome, even (especially?) when they tripped off liberal Jewish tongues.

At the same time, however, I suspect that Ellison suffered deeper grief, because his noble words about the double-sidedness of the American experience sounded a conciliatory note out of joint with the times. Bad enough that *Invisible Man* was the trump card every black novelist had to beat for mainstream recognition or that whole paragraphs from Ellison's essays were dragged out and quoted by liberal white critics, the black aesthetic movement made a case for a distinctive modus operandi that must have made Ellison shiver.

As Howe pointed out in yet another postscript to his original essay, this time when it appeared between the covers of his *Selected Writing, 1950-1990*: "In the quarter-century since this essay was written there appeared the 'black aesthetic' movement, claiming that works of literature by black writers adhere to a distinctive aesthetic and, in the more extreme versions of this outlook, that such works can be fully accessible only to black critics and readers." No matter that a hamfisted critic like Addison Gayle, the movement's chief architect and theoretician, hardly deserves mention in the same breath with subtle thinkers like Ellison and Howe, or that Don L. Lee's poetry mau-maued its way into anthologies of the time by combining a clenched fist with a screed of hate speech—the sad fact of the matter is that neither Howe nor Ellison had the in-your-face militancy that the new age required. Consigned to the ash heap of history, what could Howe say a quarter-century after he and Ellison first locked horns about a black writer's "proper" subject? One possibility, of course, is to replay the chess moves that, at best, ended in stalemate and at worst added up to something less than his finest hour. Hence, the interest in *anything* Ellison might have to say about white writers, and the note of "Yes, but . . ." that ends the piece on a curiously suspended note.

And yet (with Irving, there was always an "And yet. . ."), what may finally matter is the choice to include "Black Boys and Native Sons" among his collective essays. For if he had felt that his arguments were wrongheaded or that the case made in Ellison's series of rejoinders was insurmountable, I suspect Howe might have done otherwise. But he must have retained a faith in his arguments and in the judgment that history would eventually pass on them. At the moment his words are not likely to be treated with much kindness, either by the most militant of black students who refuse to believe, on the most misguided of principle, that no white critic—much less a white teacher—has anything of value to say to them, or by those in the academy who would write off Irving's essay as shockingly undertheorized. But then again, Ellison would not fare any better. What has not changed, however, is the fact that Howe's "Negro Problem"—like Podhoretz's and Trilling's and Mailer's—remains *ours*; and that all of us, black and white, would do well to remember how serious persons once dared to talk about the difficult, vexing matter of race. For when W. E. B. Dubois argued that the color line was the problem of the twentieth century, he was surely right; he was only wrong in failing to realize that it would also be the problem of the twenty-first.

Spike Lee: Protest, Literary Tradition, and the Individual Filmmaker

> The failure of the protest novel lies in its rejection of life, the human being, the denial of his beauty, dread, power, in its insistence that it is his categorization alone which is real and which cannot be transcended.
>
> —James Baldwin

Writing in the pages of *Partisan Review* some forty years ago James Baldwin set out to boldly link Harriet Beecher Stowe's *Uncle Tom's Cabin* with Richard Wright's *Native Son*, and to announce his separate, aesthetic peace from both. He called his essay "Everybody's Protest Novel," making it clear that the "everybody" did not include *him*:

> . . . unless one's ideal of society is a race of neatly analyzed, hard-working ciphers, one can hardly claim for the protest novels the lofty purpose they claim for themselves or share the present optimism concerning them. They emerge for what they are: a mirror of our confusion, dishonesty, panic, trapped and immobilized in the sunlit prison of the American dream.

For better or worse, protest "literature" now resides less in the novel than in rap music, street poets, and not least of all, in the films of people like Spike Lee. But Baldwin's words about a lofty purpose degenerating into images of our confusion, dishonesty, and panic still apply. In this regard, nothing has been more debated about, worried over, and lavishly overpraised than Spike Lee's "Do the Right Thing." Not only does it have the look and feel of the "streets," but it also so adroitly combines the ear-jarring insistences of Public Enemy's "Fight the Power" with paeons to the militant philosophy of Malcolm X that it might well be thought of—as Wright's *Native Son* was in its day—as "everybody's protest film."

Yet, even here—in a film designed more with an eye toward self-promotion than to "protest"—the old battle lines that divided Baldwin from Wright and Ellison from Howe remain firmly etched in the concrete of Spike Lee's Brooklyn streets. The difference, of course, is that we have so long been accustomed to feckless Hollywood films and the shoddy language that generally accompanies them (the *Sight & Sound* crowd, semioticians all, are an exception, but notable only for those who have forever abandoned clear thought and readable prose) that we have forgotten what it was like when real intellectuals do polemical battle. In short, most reviews imagine that Spike Lee's films are *sui generis*. Nothing, in fact, could be farther from the truth.

Here, for example, from an article entitled "Black Boys and Native Sons" is Irving Howe, caught in the curious position of defending Wright's clenched-fisted, uncompromising militancy, as he tries to explain—with as much sympathy and eloquence he can muster—why it is that purely aesthetic considerations must sometimes give way to the urgencies of political realities. "What, then, was the experience of a man with a black skin, what *could* it be in this country? How could a Negro put pen to paper, how could he so much as think or breathe, without some impulsion to protest, be it harsh or mild, political or private, released or buried? The 'sociology' of his experience formed a constant pressure on his literary work, and not merely in the way this might be true for any writer, but with a pain and a ferocity that nothing can remove."

Thus, protest literature—like the blues—is the black artist's congenial turf, simultaneously his or her authentic voice and delimiting condition. To his enduring credit, Ellison (then and now) has refused to credential such a vision. Rather, he argues, in "The World and the Jug,"—an essay matching Howe's thought for thought, elegant phrase for elegant phrase—that black life in America is *not* an abstraction—the "embodiment of living hell" that those who would champion protest (Wright, Howe, and now, Spike Lee) reduce it to—but, rather, "a *discipline*—just as any human life which has endured so long is a discipline teaching its own insights into the human condition, its own strategies of survival. There is a fullness, even a richness here; and here *despite* the realities of politics . . . perhaps, because it is *human* life. . . . To deny in the interest of revolutionary posture that such possibilities of human richness exist for others . . . is not only to deny us our humanity but to betray the critic's commitment to social reality."

One wants desperately to keep faith with Ellison's manifesto, to see one's race, ethnic origin, or religion as a significant "part" of a person's identity, point-of-view, essential Self, and yet, somehow, not the whole definition, not *all*; but even in the years (1963-64) when Howe and Ellison conducted their brilliant debate in the pages of *Dissent* and *The New Leader* there was little enough cause for optimism. Now there is a good deal less, not only in terms of how much more impatience has accumulated over the last twenty-five years or how mob rage now has become a staple of television's evening news, but also in terms of how voices of reason on both sides of the racial divide are in such short supply. Nobody need belabor the point that artists of Ellison's calibre are *always* a rarity, but a case can, yea, *must*, be made for artists who share something of his aesthetic commitment, his discipline to his craft, to the truth, and, perhaps, most of all, to a promise of American life more compassionate, more humane, more just than a battle royal conducted with epiphets and baseball bats.

I should also mention that, for all their differences, one of the things that Howe and Ellison shared were the same books, the same respect for the suppleness of intellectual debate, the same passion for ideas and the ways that they matter deeply in the quotidian world. This does not mean that either man was thus spared the pangs of conscience that inevitably arise when subsequent events turn even the most brilliant of arguments awry. Howe, for example, has no doubt had occasion to regret the initial enthusiasm that caused him to print Norman Mailer's "The White Negro" (1957) in the pages of *Dissent*. No doubt there are those who would argue that the essay remains a dazzling piece of social criticism/philosophy—Mailer, when he is not a "charmer" or our oldest *enfant terrible*, is something of a professional *dazzler*—but my complaint has less to do with how dusty, how intellectually threadbare and pretentious talk about "hipstersdom" seems now, but, rather, with how dangerous, and glibly dangerous at that, the argument was at its very core:

> The psychopath murders—if he has the courage—out of the necessity to purge his violence, for if he cannot empty his hatred then he cannot love, his being is frozen with implacable self-hatred for his cowardice. (It can of course be suggested that it takes little courage for two strong eighteen-year-old hoodlums, let us say, to beat in the brains of a candy-store keeper, and indeed

> the act—even by the logic of the psychopath—is not likely to prove very therapeutic, for the victim is not an immediate equal. Still, courage of a sort is necessary, for one murders not only a weak fifty-year-old man but an institution as well). . . .

Courage, of course, is one of those words that tend to get used in slippery ways, and that gives hindsight the whole show. My hunch is that Mailer does not feel the same giddy inclination to wax philosophical—in a mish-mash of Existentialism and half-digested Hemingway—after the Jack Abbot affair; and I feel even more confident that Howe, realizing the high probability that this "fifty-year-old candy store keeper" is Jewish, would not likely give his editorial approval to a similar piece today.

What concerns me, however, is that Spike Lee would have little trouble understanding how it is that murdering an elderly, rather pathetic candy store owner represents "fighting the Power," and how it is that, in Mailer's words, as one "violates private property, one enters into a new relation with the police and introduces a dangerous element into one's life." In all the ink spilled about "Do the Right Thing"—ranging from detailed discussions of cinematographer Ernest Dickerson's use of color and camera angle to speculations about whether or not the film would lead inevitably to urban riots—no reviewer has pointed out the "tradition," as it were, in which Spike Lee now numbers himself. For he, like Mailer before him, has an affinity for violence—as dangerous, as defining, as decisive—that has been the special weakness of intellectuals and artists since at least the French Revolution. On this point, Paul Johnson's recent study, *Intellectuals,* is not wrong.

Perhaps now is as good a time as any to introduce a word that crops up all too frequently in academic circles—namely, *privilege.* Used almost exclusively as a verb, along with its second-cousin "privileging," it *signifies* (another fashionable word one runs into at faculty parties) pretty much what Public Enemy means when they rap on about "the Power." Them that's got it, got it, and them that don't, don't. But that much said, it would be hard to think of a filmmaker *more* "privileged" than Spike Lee has been (his family not only footed the bills at N.Y.U.'s film school, but also scraped up the enormous cash necessary to produce his first film—"She's gotta Have It") and less like the street blacks who provide both his persona and his audience. Nor would it be easy to find a young filmmaker more overpraised than Mr. Lee. Everything about his work—but especially the uncompromising militancy, the stick-it-to-whitey posture in "Do the Right Thing"—brings out superlatives from liberal critics in roughly the same way that the death of Little Eva made Harriet Beecher Stowe's Victorian readers gush. In neither case are the emotions earned; rather they are merely insisted upon. There is, in short, something intellectually soft and all too predictable in Lee's latest films.

In Stowe's case at least there are reasons to believe her sincerity, if not to entirely trust her product (she claimed, after all, that God—and not Harriet Beecher Stowe—had really written *Uncle Tom's Cabin*). Spike Lee would hardly make a similar pronouncement. Despite the Power, despite Hollywood's timidity, despite racism itself, *he* prevailed. In a word, it is Spike Lee who is now "privileged." To the victor goeth the spoils: phone calls enthusiastically returned; projects foisted upon him; interviews, photo opportunities, the Whole Works. For a fistful of hard cash one can buy t-shirts, baseball caps, and assorted Spike Lee momentos at "Spike's Joint," his newly-owned emporium in the Brooklyn where his films are shot. If these were merely personal aberrations they would not matter (after all, one does not have to admire the artist to admire his or her art), but in Lee's case the sophomoric displays of pique spill over onto the silver screen.

Given the shameful history of Hollywood's treatment of blacks, much of this attention is a just cause for celebration. Spike Lee *does* have talent, and I would be the last one to urge him to be subservient in an industry where funding requires one to be ever more aggressive about box-office appeal and increasingly conventional with regard to one's art. It's not an easy act to balance, and it never was. But when privilege turns out to be an opportunity to make television commercials for Nike sneakers—however interesting or witty they, in fact, are—one has the right to ask if the enemy Spike Lee is so anxious to overthrow is not, in fact, staring back at him from the mirror. Although the word has rather gone out of fashion of late, the term I'm groping for is "co-opted." Granted, the hard cash from Nike—which is no doubt considerable, and no doubt well-earned given Spike Lee's high visibility with young blacks—will allow him to make more films along the lines of "Do the Right Thing." But for those old enough to remember, that argument is remarkably similar to the one university deans used during the late 1960s when they explained that the federal dollars sponsoring "secret research" in the biology department freed up money for a new theatre building—and, moreover, that the drama department could put on as many anti-War plays as it wished. The argument didn't wash in their mouths, and it is no more compelling in Spike Lee's.

The bald fact, of course, is that Nike's are as much a symbol as they are a product—and here one can cite "Do the Right Think" itself as Exhibit A. When an uppity white boy (wearing a Celtic's shirt no less) inadvertently tracks his bicycle treads over Buggin' Out's (Giancarlo Esposito) lily white sneakers, his indignation is as comic (credit one point to Mr. Lee) as it is heartfelt. Buggin' Out has what used to be known as a short fuse; he looks for confrontational situations as if it were a full-time occupation. And not surprisingly, he finds them, although in this case, it is Buggin' Out who blinks when the going starts getting tough (another point for Mr. Lee). At this juncture, however, it is hard to tell the Spike Lee who has a sharp eye for satirizing black life (as he clearly, and with something of a mean spirit, does in "School Daze") from the Spike Lee whose commercials for Nike can only make a bad socioeconomic situation worse.

More imaginative artists, both black and white, have had larger souls, more compassion, a wider vision. Writing at a time when Jim Crow laws were being passed and the Klan dominated the newspapers of that day every bit as much as Bensonhurst does in our time, Mark Twain—a man at least as well acquainted with racism as Mr. Lee—wrote about an ignorant slum kid named Huck, an escaped Slave named Jim, and a raft:

> Other places do seem so cramped and smothery, but a raft don't. You feel mighty free and easy and comfortable on a raft. . . . Soon as it was night, out we shoved; when we got her out to about the middle, we let her alone, and let her float wherever the current wanted her to; then we lit our pipes, and dangled our legs in the water and talked about all kinds of things—we was always naked, day and night, whenever the mosquitoes would let us—. . . . It's lovely to live on a raft.

In that idyll on the Mississippi—more than an Edenic match for the syrup "Driving Miss Daisy" pours across the silver screen—is not only one of our most powerful archetypes, but also a vision of democratic possibility. That it is under constant threat—like the raft which must contend with currents, with steamboats, and most of all, with scallawags such as the Duke and the King—is true enough, for at its deepest level *Adventures of Huckleberry*

Finn is a sad, even heart-breaking book. Yet, one must ask if the lessons that bind Huck to Jim, that prompt him to risk an eternal damnation (which *he* fully believes will be his fate for aiding-and-abetting a slave, even though we, as Twain's readers, know better and cheer our hero's defiance on), are worth nothing? If ever there was a "protest novel" about everything that is ugly and pernicious about racism it is *Adventures of Huckleberry Finn*. Nor does the fact that racism, more than a hundred years later, persists as *the* American problem lessen Twain's achievement. Nor does it diminish the brave words of Ellison's protagonist who, despite his "invisibility," struggles to keep faith with the promises of a democratic America, rather than with those, black or white, who would subvert those principles and thus reduce him to a cipher, a symbol, a "thing" to be pulled up or, more often, pushed down. As Ellison put it when he received the National Book Award in 1953, because American life was too vital and alive to be caught by the Jamesian novel and because what we usually think of as the protest novel was too dependent on "physical violence, social cynicism, and understatement," he found himself

> . . . turning to our classical nineteenth-century novelists. I felt that except for the work of William Faulkner something vital had gone out of American prose after Mark Twain. I came to believe that the writers of that period took a much greater responsibility for the condition of democracy and, indeed, their works were imaginative projections of the conflicts within the human heart which arose when the sacred principles of the Constitution and the Bill of Rights clashed with the practical exigencies of human greed and fear, hate and love. Naturally I was attracted to these writers as a Negro.

One wonders how many students currently attending classes in African-American studies programs have been assigned these words—not only the parts about a writer's responsibility for the "condition of democracy" and the parts that echo Faulkner's pronouncements—from "The Bear" and, later, his Nobel Prize Acceptance Speech—about the human heart in conflict with itself, but perhaps even more important than these, the implications of Ellison's last line?

By contrast, Spike Lee makes much of the oppressive heat that glares off the city's sidewalks and boils inside the racist hearts that ride into black neighborhoods to rip off its pizza-hungry citizens yet one more day. But one wonders if Mr. Lee has paid as much attention to, say, William Faulkner's story "Dry September" as he has to imagining how the *New York Post*'s banner headline might look. Albert Camus, whose *The Stranger* makes it clear that he also knows something about the effects that heat can have on a character such as Mersaualt, once characterized Faulkner's world as one of "heat and dust"; what similar words might apply to Mookie's—heat and hatred? My point is simply that Spike Lee's films settle for the surface, and for the superficial. One learns something important about the psychodynamics of a lynch mob in Faulkner's story—something that digs deeply into the racist mentality and produces the emotions of pity and fear that were central to classical tragedy; and in his finest achievements—*The Sound and the Fury, Absalom, Absalom!, Light in August*—those emotions come to us with a force that first surprises and then convinces. I, for one, do not find much that ties "Do the Right Thing" into a similarly convincing package—not the Sal who insists on paying the same Mookie who precipitated the dismantling of his pizzeria and certainly not the pretense that the quotations from Martin Luther King, Jr. and Malcolm X that roll across the screen at the end have been dramatized with equal weight.

Among the things that make "Do the Right Thing" so *au courant* are the easy ways it accepts the failure of a democratic America as a fact and racial hatred as inevitability. Indeed, the best "justice" the film can offer is a chance for blacks, white cops, and Korean grocers to get equal time as each in turn stares into the camera and unleashes a string of racial epiphets.

"Do the Right Thing" asks us to "Fight the Power," but not only is the "Power" *not* Sal, it is the glib way that Spike Lee turns it into a convenient symbol that gives me the willies. For when an artist loses touch with human beings—taken one by one, black or white—bad Art and dangerous Ideas are sure to follow. And in "Do the Right Thing"—for all its illusion of "community"—Mookie strikes me as an isolated character: in the scenes with his girlfriend Tina (Rosie Perez) and his essentially fatherless child; in his endless squabbles with his sister Jade; indeed, in the very way that his job as a delivery boy allows simultaneously for movement and stasis, for Mookie fits comfortably into neither Sal's world (just ask Pino [John Turturro], Sal's virulently racist son) nor the world into which Sal's customers will enter when they graduate, and that Spike Lee had already devastated in "School Daze."

Again, what Baldwin says about *Native Son*—in "Many Thousands Gone"—can, with a pinch here, a tuck there, be applied to "Do the Right Thing":

> What the novel reflects—and at no point interprets—is the isolation of the Negro within his own group and the resulting fury of impatient scorn. It is this which creates its climate of anarchy and unmotivated and unapprehending disaster; and it is this climate, common to most Negro protest novels, which has led us all to believe that in Negro life there exists no tradition, no field of manners, no possibility of ritual or intercourse, such as may, for example, sustain the Jew even after he has left his father's house. But the fact is not that the Negro has no tradition but that there has as yet arrived no sensibility sufficiently profound and tough enough to make this tradition articulate. For a tradition expresses, after all, nothing more than the long and painful experience of a people; it comes out of the battle waged to maintain their integrity or, to put it more simply, out of their struggle to survive. When we speak of the Jewish tradition we are speaking of centuries of exile and persecution, of the strength which endured and the sensibility which discovered in it the high possibility of the moral victory.

Baldwin himself meant to be part of the new "articulate" sensibility he called for, part of a tradition that could move the crudities of the protest novel into something profoundly richer; and in some of his books, he was—as were, and are, such writers as Ellison and Toni Morrison. But Spike Lee is destined to be written down as the writer-director-actor of "everybody's protest film," and as I have tried to argue, that is no longer enough, nor was it ever enough. He will, no doubt, become yet another talk show "personality"—one known for being known—in a culture already far too crowded with such types.

That he is a black artist in a country that needs sensibility and articulate speech more than ever merely compounds the shame. For Spike Lee seems to be a man with a keener eye for generating controversy than for making coherent films. Whatever else may be said of, say, "Mo' Better Blues," it did not lack for ambition—at least according to Mr. Lee. As a film about jazz and jazz musicians, "Mo' Better Blues" aimed to demolish the competition; and not only such recent efforts as Clint Eastwood's "Bird" or Bertrand Tavernier's "'Round Midnight," but also everything from "Man With the Golden Arm" onward. Unfortunately, the center of "Mo' Better Blues" does not hold. At what *should* be its center is Bleek Gilliam (Denzel Washington), a man obsessed enough with his trumpet to suffer all for his Art. That he is a significant cut below the genius of, say, a Charles Mingus is presumably less important than the fact that Bleek—a matinee idol if there ever was one—is caught between two women (one a schoolteacher, the other an aspiring singer) who compete for his attention and who, taken together, represent a threat to his practice time. If all this sounds vaguely familiar, it is—for Hollywood has been churning out similar froth for decades.

What Lee adds, of course, are black faces, and a less-than-subtle thesis about the exploitation of black musicians. The issue, in short, comes down to control, or if you wish, to *power*. And in "Mo' Better Blues," the pursestrings are in the tight-fisted, altogether despicable hands of Moe and Josh Flatbush (John and Nicholas Turturro). No matter that Bleek's manager, Giant (Spike Lee) is inept or that he cares more about placing a bet than he does about looking out for Bleek's best interests; no matter that the track record of Jewish managers and black musicians is decidedly better than Lee's film implies; and finally, no matter that black faces are conspicuously absent in the crowd where Bleek performs—what makes it tough for a good looker like Bleek Gilliam are whiteys, and Jewish whiteys in particular.

Not surprisingly, the *New York Times* soon crackled with accusations about anti-Semitism and then with counter-charges by Spike Lee himself: "I'm not a racist; I'm not a bigot; I am not an anti-Semite [he wrote in an August 22, 1990, op-ed piece]. What I try to do with all my characters is offer what I feel are honest portraits of individuals with both faults and endearing characteristics." True enough for, say, the embattled Sal of "Do the Right Thing," but for the Flatbush brothers of "Mo' Better Blues"? Hardly. Indeed, to find its equal one would have to look not to Hollywood, but to the rough-and-tumble vaudeville stage at the turn of the century (where grotesque portraitures of drunken Irishmen, shuffling blacks, and dishonest Jews brought down the house) or to the hate-mongering of demagogues like Gerald L. K. Smith and Father Coughlin.

Sadly, Lee seems more interested in establishing his right to portray Jews or Italians as negatively as he wishes. And not surprisingly, he takes white directors to task when blacks appear in their films as pimps or drug addicts—this despite the fact that "Jungle Fever," unlike Lee's earlier efforts, includes shots of a less-than-squeaky-clean Harlem and a black crackhead. No doubt Lee would argue that *his* drug addict is more *character* than stereotype, but I suspect there are those in Bensonhurst who saw stereotypes a'plenty in "Jungle Fever" and that they did not especially enjoy the film's heavy handed Italian-bashing. The point, of course, is that caricature is caricature—whether the object happens to be black or Jewish or Italian. Moreover, with Spike Lee there is a further point—namely, that he remains more interested in "exposure" than he is in creating anything that a Baldwin or an Ellison would recognize as Art. The recent release of "Malcolm X" makes it clear, once again, that Lee's work is the very stuff of controversy—long on hoopla and ink, short on awards. Not surprisingly, Lee blames the Academy of Motion Picture Arts and Sciences for preferring "Scent of a Woman" to "Malcolm X" and insists that his film will last in ways that Pacino's performance will not. Perhaps. But what is clear is that Lee's epic about Malcolm X is longer on dutifulness than delight, and that it tells us more about the passions of the moment than it does about the aesthetic requirements of a well-made, well-edited film.

Magic Realism, Historical Truth, and the Quest for a Liberating Identity: Reflections on Alex Haley's *Roots* and Toni Morrison's *Song of Solomon*

> There are events that really happen and afterwards become legends, and there are legends which afterwards become events; there are no boundaries between reality and dreams, between reality and fiction, between what is seen and what is imagined. The magic of our climate and light gives our stories a double aspect—from one side they seem dreams, from the other, realities.
>
> —Miguel Angel Asturias

The patterns of Ralph Ellison's *Invisible Man* are vertical rather than horizontal, finally more concerned with descent and re-emergence than with prolonged explorations into History. Nameless at the beginning of his odyssey through a wide assortment of "definitions" and adjustments—everything from "education" in the Booker T. Washington mode to the competing claims of communism and black nationalism—he is equally nameless at the end. What he has learned is the undeniable, palpable fact of his invisibility. Whatever nagging questions remain (how to interpret correctly, and act courageously on, his grandfather's deathbed advice), it seems clear that the "socially useful role" an invisible man can play is none other than to write the book we have just finished. And like Joyce's God of creation, Ellison remains within or behind or beyond or above his handiwork, paring his fingernails in Joyce's case or inscribing both archetype and signature on the title-page in Ellison's.

For more years than many of us care to remember, Ellison's novel loomed as an intimidating presence, not only because of its dazzling blend of folkloric elements and High Art, but also because it became the benchmark against which the work of successive black novelists would be judged. *Invisible Man* became, in a word, an eminently "teachable" book—

thoroughly respectable, thoroughly domesticated, and, despite its dogged efforts at universalism, thoroughly anchored in a literary milieu that loved myth and symbol, irony and the New Criticism above all else.

Alex Haley's *Roots* changed everything—not because it "advanced" black fiction by being more innovative, more technically daring than *Invisible Man* (indeed, Ishmael Reed had been more experimental-than-thou for years, and with negligible results), but because it purported, unashamedly and old-fashionedly, to "instruct and delight" black Americans about the historical truth. Unlike Ellison's complicated narrative recollected in the underground, Haley sees History as chronological lines: one beginning with Kunta Kinte's birth ("Early in the spring of 1750, in the village of Juffure, four days upriver from the coast of The Gambia, West Africa . . ."[1]) and moving forward; the other beginning with Alex Haley's nagging questions about his ancestors, the bits of information he collects, the dogged research he does, and moving backward. In Haley's case, the figure in the carpet, the Rosetta Stone, the Missing Link, is less the literary imagination than it is his discovery of the right *griot*:

> The old *griot* [oral historian] had talked for nearly two hours up to then, and perhaps fifty times the narrative had included some detail about someone whom he had named. Now after he had just named those four sons, [Kunta, Lamin, Suwadu, and Madi], again he appended a detail, and the interpreter translated—
>
> "About the time the King's soldiers came"—another of the *griot*'s time-fixing references—"the eldest of these four sons, Kunta, went away from his village to chop wood . . . and he was never seen again. . . ."
>
> I sat as if I were carved of stone. My blood seemed to have congealed. This man whose lifetime had been in this back-country African village had no way in the world to know that he had just echoed what I had heard all through my boyhood years on my grandma's front porch in Henning, Tennessee . . . of an African who always insisted that his name was "Kin-tay"; who had called a guitar a "*ko*," and a river within the state of Virginia, "Kamby Bolongo"; and who had been kidnapped into slavery while not far from his village, chopping wood, to make himself a drum. (578-79)

I have quoted Haley at length because *Roots* moves relentlessly toward authentication, toward that "epiphany" in which Kunta Kinte's long-lost "son" at last comes home. By now, of course, the saga of Kunta Kinte's family has moved, via print and television, into the national consciousness, as a historical chronicle begun in the libraries of the record-keeping West and ended in the long sweep of an oral historian/storyteller. And, as such, it takes its place among those national types that readers and non-readers alike share: a penniless, disheveled Benjamin Franklin walking through the streets of Philadelphia with "three great Puffy rolls"; a log-cabin-born, rail-splitting Abe Lincoln more than holding his own in the great debates over slavery; John Fitzgerald Kennedy at the helm of the PT-109. To be sure, in recovering the truth about Kunta Kinte, Haley was speaking for, and to, other black Americans who might launch their own searches or, if not that, at least know that they *could*:

> . . . *if* any black American could be so blessed as I had been to know only a few ancestral clues—could he or she know *who* was either the paternal or maternal African ancestor or ancestors, and about *where* that ancestor lived when taken, and finally about *when* the ancestor was taken—then only those few clues might well see that black American able to locate some wizened old black *griot* whose narrative could reveal the black American's ancestral clan, perhaps even the very village. (579-80)

To the question—posed, now and then, as Haley lectured about the book during its twelve years of gestation—"How much of *Roots* is fact and how much is fiction?" he is confident, unequivocal:

> To the best of my knowledge and of my effort, every lineage statement within *Roots* is from either my African or American families' carefully preserved oral history, much of which I have been able conventionally to corroborate with documents. Those documents, along with the myriad textual details of what were contemporary indigenous lifestyles, cultural history, and such that give *Roots* flesh have come from years of intensive research in fifty-odd libraries, archives, and other repositories on three continents. (584)

The aftermath of *Roots* was another matter: Haley settled one lawsuit for plagiarism, but academic juries are still out where other matters of fact—including the *griot* in whom Haley vested so much faith—are concerned. For Leslie Fiedler, the debate about historical veracity is not only pointless, but something of a mug's game because

> . . . *all* contributions to our inadvertent prose epic [i.e. that saga of unending black-white struggle in America fashioned from *Uncle Tom's Cabin, Birth of a Nation, Gone With the Wind,* and *Roots*] have claimed to be

> more truth than fantasy. . . . Not just the works of Mrs. Stowe and Dixon, D. W. Griffith and Margaret Mitchell, but the Slave Narratives and White histories of Reconstruction on which they drew were, to one degree or another, fictional constructs.[2]

I have no especial quarrel with Fiedler's subtle and all-embracing notion of "fictional constructs," but there is some obligation, I think, to point out that the mass audience so dear to Fiedler's heart *does*. For them, *Roots* was made of sterner stuff than *Uncle Tom's Cabin* or *Gone With the Wind*; it was historically accurate, verifiable, True. Otherwise, *Roots* would be just another "novel," which is to say, just another pack of lies. At this point, a bit of literary history may be helpful. Since the publication of Truman Capote's *In Cold Blood* (1966) and Norman Mailer's *Armies of the Night* (1968), the line dividing fiction from nonfiction has become increasingly blurred.[3] And while the New Journalism (now somewhat old, and even predictable) has raised the level of journalistic writing to dizzying stylistic heights, it has reduced—at times obliterated—the obligations that their respective material demands of the fictionalist and the historian. If, as Mailer's slash would have it, "novel as history/history as novel" is the new dispensation, much can fall conveniently between the cracks: the novelist need not be entirely faithful to an imaginative vision, to aesthetic norms, because "documentation" presumably takes up the slack; likewise, the historian need not be entirely faithful to the facts because the "fiction" so demands. In this way a writer receives the benefits of both, without enduring the responsibilities of either.

Roots surely benefited from this recent turn of literary circumstances, although I hasten to point out that any similarities between Haley's wooden writing and the breathtaking stylists I cited in the previous paragraph are strictly accidental. Here is a representative sample, taken from Kunta Kinte's first impression of captivity:

> Kunta wondered if he had gone mad. Naked, chained, shackled, he awoke on his back between two other men in a pitch darkness full of steamy heat and sickening stink and a nightmarish bedlam of shrieking, weeping, praying, and vomiting. He could feel and smell his own vomit on his chest and belly. His whole body was one spasm of pain from the beatings he had received in the four days since his capture. But the place where the hot iron had been put between his shoulders hurt the worst. (127)

The hackneyed word choices are, of course, perfect fodder for translation into television, which, of course, is exactly what happened to them. But, as Fiedler insists, there is another, more important energy at work in *Roots*: "Haley possesses, though perhaps only by fits and starts, that mythopoeic power which neither ineptness of language nor banality of ideas can impugn" (231). To be sure, by "mythopoeic power," Fiedler means sadomasochism in sentimental garb, means that *Roots*, like *Gone With the Wind*, energizes black-white relations in ways that our uneasy dreams whisper about but which, in our fully conscious lives, we dare not admit. Perhaps . . . but I suspect the issue is simpler by half than Fiedler's ingenuity dares admit. For what we have in *Roots* is, first, a name and a legacy—Kunta Kinte—that provides a model of dignity, continuity, and pride and, then, a family chronicle that stands four-square against everything in the sad history of American life which would destroy it. One would have to go back to Cotton Mather's *Magnalia Christi Americana* to find its equal in portraits of edification and uplift. In this sense, *Roots* is a quintessentially American book, its publication during the hoopla of the Bicentennial less the happy accident Haley claims or the clever marketing ploy his detractors suspect, but precisely the destiny the book deserves. And if the fever for establishing one's geneology has died down among blacks as well as other ethnic groups in America, it will, no doubt, return. That, of course, is to talk *sociologically* which is proper for a book like *Roots*. It is rather like speculating about the impact that writing for both *The Reader's Digest* and *Playboy Magazine* might have had on the twin strands of official piety and purient sensationalism one finds in *Roots*—interesting literary gossip, stabs at understanding the creative process, but little more. What matters about *Roots* is not its enormous popular success or even the second thoughts, reservations, controversies, or renewed popularity it may experience, but the sadder realization—for all Fiedler's insistence about popular culture's grip—that no imagination, black or white, can be liberated for long, or perhaps at all, by such a hackneyed vision, by such a badly written work.

A novel with a much greater chance for the kind of liberation I have in mind arrived, curiously enough, a scant year after *Roots* threatened to elbow serious black fiction out of the marketplace entirely. It, too, was about a search for beginnings, a quest to re-discover one's *name* and what it means, but its metaphor was soaring flight and its style was "magical." I use the last term to suggest the kinship between Toni Morrison's *Song of Solomon* and the "magical realism" of South American writers like Gabriel García Márquez (*One Hundred Years of Solitude*), however much separates them geographically and politically. But in the intermingling of the fantastic and the realistic, the fragmentations of plot, the penchant for kaleidoscopic dissolves, the sheer dazzle of language that evokes fairy tale at one level and family chronicle at another, these writers share much with each other. Most importantly of all, they are committed to a postmodernist aesthetic that, in Morrison's case, means a substantial departure from the modernist assumptions of *Invisible Man*.

Song of Solomon is a triumph of flight, of transcendence, framed by its curiously disarming opening sentence ("The North Carolina Mutual Life Insurance agent promised to fly from Mercy to the other side of Lake Superior at three o'clock") and Macon ("Milkman") Dead's ambivalent final gesture (suicidal? surrendering? life-affirming? mystically transcendent?):

> Milkman stopped waving and narrowed his eyes . . . he leaped. As fleet and bright as a lodestar he wheeled toward Guitar [his potential killer] and it did not matter which one of them would give up his ghost in the killing arms of his brother. For now he knew what Shalimar knew: If you surrendered to the air, you could *ride* it. (337)

To know what Shalimar knew—indeed, to know anything, finally and deeply—is at the heart of *Song of Solomon*'s vision, and its "style." In her earlier novels (*The Bluest Eye* [1970] and *Sula* [1973]), critics singled out Morrison's "language" for special praise, usually by way of indicating that it was haunting, strangely compelling, "poetic." Generally speaking, this means the reviewer, however much he or she *liked* the novel, was somewhat baffled about what, precisely, to say. Equating such novels with poetry is as honorific as it is safe. Nonetheless, there is a sense in which the prose in *Song of Solomon* works on several levels simultaneously, a sense in which quotidian reality is temporarily suspended. That, I submit, is what happens as one reads the novel's opening sentence. We do not yet know that Mercy refers to a hospital; indeed, it is the deeper meanings of "mercy"—in all its ironic starkness—that work on our unconscious. Gradually, very gradually, Morrison sketches in the details and, more importantly, the public history that underpins them. We learn, for example, that Mains Avenue had an alternate reality among the black population as Doctor Street, because "the only colored doctor in the city had lived and died on that street." When post office workers refused to deliver letters addressed to "Doctor Street" (Mains Avenue, after all, was on the map while Doctor Street existed only in the mind), the Dead Letter Office became one muscle in the long arm of the law; and when city legislators posted notices that the street "had always been and would always be known as Mains Avenue and not Doctor Street," that was another. The street people, of course, knew better, and in a victory of mind over institutional matter, they called it Not Doctor Street.

Robert Smith's suicide note announces the exact time and date of his "flight" as if he were a stuntman, a pitchman in the P. T. Barnum tradition: "At 3:00 p.m. on Wednesday the 18th of February 1931, I will take off from Mercy and fly away on my own wings" (3). Present time in the chronological sweep of Macon Dead and his bizarre family begins at this point:

> When the dead doctor's daughter [Ruth Foster Dead] saw Mr. Smith emerge as promptly as he had promised from behind the cupola, his wide blue silk wings curved forward around his chest, she dropped her covered peck basket, spilling red velvet rose petals. The wind blew them about, up, down, and into small mounds of snow. Her half-grown daughters scrambled about trying to catch them, while their mother moaned and held the underside of her stomach. The rose-petal scramble got a lot of attention, but the pregnant lady's moans did not. (5)

Smith's blue silk cape has the imagistic force of a cocoon, albeit one that "curved forward around his chest" like a shroud. In *his* case, he "leaped on into the air" and his death. The swirling, and artificial, rose petals prefigure Smith's "fall" but, more importantly, Milkman's birth. The chaotic events of February 18, 1931, lead directly to his sense of inherited "specialness," not only because he was the first black admitted to the hospital they called, significantly, No Mercy, but also because Milkman "discovered, at four, the same thing Mr. Smith had learned earlier—that only birds and airplanes could fly. . . . To have to live without that single gift saddened him and left his imagination so bereft that he appeared dull even to the women who did not hate his mother" (9). Macon Dead, known as "Milkman" because he nursed "long after he was old enough to be bored by the flat taste of his mother's milk" and yet too young to be dazzled sexually by her nipples, is the center of consciousness amid a family that looks for all the world like the House of Atreus set down in Michigan and made up in blackface. His father drives relentlessly toward money, toward property, toward anything that will blot out his mysterious past and shore up the respectability of his future; his mother keeps her faith with her aristocratic, doctor father, desperately seeking the love her tooth-clenched husband has denied her. Add a generous selection of exotic minor characters with names like First Corinthians and Pilate, and the equipoise between surface texture and heightened fancy we know as "magical realism" seems complete.

In this general sense, Morrison seems closer to Ellison than Haley. But in *Song of Solomon*, the folkloric elements strike us as more natural—that is, less artificially imposed on the text as clanking literary symbols—than they do in *Invisible Man*. The confusion about Not Doctor Street is simply one instance of competing notions of reality, of how we "call" the world around us. Morrison's novel bursts with such instances of suspended reality, of that "naming" so essential to an Adamic vision. R. W. B. Lewis's *The American Adam* insists that this is a special preoccupation of our literature, the natural consequence of giving shape and meaning to a virgin landscape. And we are hardly surprised when quintessentially American protagonists call themselves Christopher Newman or Nick Adams, or when the rhetoric of *The Great Gatsby*'s final page takes the following turn:

> . . . for a transitory enchanted moment man must have held his breath in the presence of this continent, compelled into an aesthetic contemplation he neither understood nor desired, face to face for the last time in history with something commensurate to his capacity for wonder.

There is no need to rehearse the central importance of these lines to any discussion of the American Dream—no writer, before or since, has understood, and lived out, its tragic dimensions more deeply that F. Scott Fitzgerald. But we have not paid nearly so much attention to the lines' elegiac character: Fitzgerald articulates all that is fleeting about the American experiment, all that is destined to be reduplicated in meretriciousness and inauthenticity. Granted, we extend our admiration to those, like Gatsby, who beat on, "boats against the current"—they are, at least, far superior to the "rotten bunch" sunk into their boredom and carelessness—but the life that really shimmers is irrevocably and unrecapturably in the past. Thus was it ever written, in the modernist account of American creation.

By contrast, Morrison envisions an ongoing mythopoesis, one deeply ingrained within the fabric of black life and, ultimately, available to the likes of Milkman Dead. The "truths" of History—like the consensus reality of place names and "official" identifications—not only count for less, they are, in fact, obstacles to understanding. Names and, more importantly, learning to name one's name—to discover it, come to terms with it, embrace it—is what the quests in *Song of Solomon* are about. For Ellison's protagonist, there are false identities that he must learn to slough off, painfully, like a snake's dead skin. Literature's Great Tradition, however, is always just off-stage, pulling the symbolic strings. For Haley, there is his spiritual kinship with Kunta Kinte that must be authenticated. In his case, the library stacks confirm what he had only dimly suspected. Morrison embraces simultaneously the collective experience of outsiders in an American ethos, and the special richness that black life in America can create. Milkman, for example, learns about the lineage of the "Dead" in a series of confrontations, and by dint of his own questing detective work. At one point, Milkman's father puts it this way:

> Everything bad that ever happened to him [Macon Dead, Milkman's grandfather] happened because he couldn't read. Got his name messed up cause he couldn't read. . . . [A functionary at the Freedman's Bureau] asked Papa where he was born. Papa said Macon. Then he asked him who his father was. Papa said, 'He's dead.' Asked him who owned him, Papa said, 'I'm free.' Well, the Yankee wrote it all down, but in the wrong spaces. Had him born in Dunfrie, wherever the hell that is, and in the space for his name the fool wrote, 'Dead' comma 'Macon." But Papa couldn't read so he never found out what he was registered as till Mama told him. (54-55)

Behind the cruel joke, the dark humor, lies the history of American immigration writ small. The convulsions of History may have made him "done free" (cf. Dunfrie) but they have also labeled him as "Dead." Milkman needs to learn both sides of this ironic Truth, and to transcend it in imaginative flight. As his father puts it, in a prophetic line that might serve as the epigraph for Morrison's novel: "'You want to be a whole man, you have to deal with the whole truth'" (76).

For Milkman, the "whole truth" means coming to terms

with a family that includes members called Pilate Dead, First Corinthians Dead, Magdalene Dead—all "names" chosen at random (?) from the family Bible, and with resonances that Morrison surely intends. If interviews are to be believed, Morrison's own mother "was named out of the Bible, the way they were in the book."[5] No doubt this is a *piece* of the truth, of the personal mythologies that contribute to an artistic effort, but *Song of Solomon* soars well beyond and above the brand of family chronicling we find in *Roots*. The names per se are as "magic," as haunting, as they are mythic. Rather than Faulkner's self-consciously "literary" choice of Joe Christmas for the sacrificial, tragic mulatto of *Light in August*, Morrison's names are more akin to those found in Gabriel García Márquez's *One Hundred Years of Solitude*. Like the Buendias, what defines one of Morrison's characters is more likely to be found in the magic of fairy tale and bizarre physiology than in the documentation, the "truth," that realistic History cares about.

For example, there is Pilate who, at twelve years of age, took her *name*—written on a piece of paper—out of the Bible, "folded it up into a tiny knot and put it in a little brass box, and strung the entire contraption through her left earlobe" (19). But that, as they say, is only the beginning of her strangeness. Her credentials as an outsider were firmly established at her birth: ". . . her stomach was as smooth and sturdy as her back, at no place interrupted by a navel" (27). Without a navel, which is to say without "connections" to the family of man, people were convinced "she had not come into this world through normal channels." She is, in fact, akin to those Heroes with dubious parentage (usually a father who is a god and a mother who conceives the child under strange, immaculate circumstances) who follow the patterns outlined in Lord Raglan's *The Hero* rather than the normal processes of the human condition.

This *touches* on Pilate, to be sure, but does not exhaust her force in the novel. If one wants to make of her smooth belly, her "inhumanness," a comment about discontinuities with the past, so be it, but that will tell you precious little about the power of Morrison's style. For style is what, again and again, works its magic on us in *Song of Solomon*. Pilate is the Life Force, in all its earthy, gritty particulars. Unlike her brother, Pilate operates (as a moonshiner) just outside the limits of the law, but she also is in close touch with the raw nerves of human feeling. As Reynolds Price points out, Milkman's journey of learning is directly related to the thwarted life he leads between his embattled parents and the Oedipal warfare they wage over him and related also to Pilate, "whose dedication to life and feeling is directly opposite her brother's methodical acquisition of things."[6] Pilate's brass box points the way, suggests a past his father resists, but Milkman must unearth its truth for himself.

Without a liberating identity—in this case, Milkman's discovery of song per se and, in particular, what the "song of Solomon" means—he is destined to languish in the aridity of a blocked heart and the dull heat of smoldering resentments:

> He just wanted to beat a path away from his parents' past, which was also their present and which was threatening to become his present as well. He hated the acridness in his mother's and father's relationship, the conviction of righteousness they each held on to with both hands. And his efforts to ignore it, transcend it, seemed to work only when he spent his days looking for whatever was light-hearted and without grave consequences. He avoided commitment and strong feelings, and shied away from decisions. (180)

This "flight," however, is doomed a priori, not only because the world of Blood Bank (filled as it is with ghetto versions of prostitutes, bullies, assorted crazies, and idle eccentrics) is one that always lies just beyond his reach—as the "Milkman," he has a long history of being set apart—but also because Milkman's destiny lies somewhere else. In effect, Blood Bank is, at best, a holding action, a place where Milkman can lick his psychic wounds before setting off into the wider, scarier world.

Initially, Milkman leaves Michigan in search of a long-hidden cache of gold—yet another installment in the family myth he receives in something like the way Quentin Compson learns about the South in Faulkner's *Absalom, Absalom!*—, but Morrison's dazzling "introductory" prose suggests that he is in for "discoveries" of a radically different kind:

> When Hansel and Gretel stood in the forest and saw the house in the clearing before them, the little hairs at the nape of their necks must have shivered. . . . No one was there to warn or hold them; their parents, chastened and grieving, were far away. . . . A grown man can also be energized by hunger, and any weakness in his knees or irregularity in his heartbeat will disappear if he thinks his hunger is about to be assuaged. Especially if the object of his craving is not gingerbread or chewy gumdrops, but gold. (219)

The image of tiny hairs standing at attention along the nape of one's neck reminds us of Emily Dickinson's definition of poetry, and it conflates the Hansel-Gretel fairy tale, with its poetry, into the more conventional saga of Milkman's gold hunt. Like the imagistically dazzling story of Robert Smith's "leap" that opens the novel, Morrison here juxtaposes realistic detail with magical resonances, teasing us with "facts" withheld and "deep images" as yet unexplored.

What Milkman discovers, in part, is that his grandfather's long-lost name was *Jake* but, more importantly, that *he* was the son of a man named Solomon who, as the song puts it, "*done fly, Solomon done gone / Solomon cut across the sky, Solomon gone home*." To be sure, I have compressed the tangled richness, the thick, ambition of Morrison's account. Milkman ventures into America in something of the way in which Marlow travels up the river—and backward in time—in Conrad's "Heart of Darkness." But if the chronological arrow of the novel moves ever inward and backward, it also arcs round to images which set *Song of Solomon* into motion: Solomon "done gone"; his son, we remember, was written down as Dunfrie—i.e., "done free." Therein lies the essential, unrecapturable difference. And, too, the "song" that Milkman discovers—and which seals his manhood—is not unlike the "song" heard on the fateful day of Smith's "flight":

> O Sugarman done fly
> O Sugarman done gone . . .
>
> Downtown the fireman pulled on their greatcoats, but when they arrived at Mercy, Mr. Smith had seen the rose petals, heard the music, and leaped on into the air. (9)

Understanding and compassion wash over Milkman. Even more importantly, he finds a deeper vein of History, one that trumps even the legacy of old Macon Dead the first: Solomon could fly! "Hating his parents, his sisters, seemed silly now," Milkman reflects, and he sets out to put aright in "magic," in the imagination, what "history" had wronged:

> He read the road signs with interest now, wondering what lay beneath the names. The Algonquins had named the territory he lived in Great Water, *michi gami*. How many dead lives and fading memories were buried in and beneath the names of the places in this country. Under the *recorded* names, just as "Macon Dead," recorded for all time in some dusty files, hid from view the real names of people, places and things. Names that had meaning. No wonder Pilate put hers

> in her car. When you know your name, you should hang on to it. . . . (329)

No wonder, too, that Alex Haley should search so methodically to find out all he could about the old African who was called, against his will, Toby. But as Morrison knows all too well, the dusty files of recorded history contain only a partial truth. Nor is it any longer enough to simply expose, as Ellison's novel so brilliantly does, the layer upon layer of false identity that blacks must pierce on the way to "invisibility." For as Morrison dramatizes (and, indeed, that is the key word, because Milkman's epiphany would count for little if were so much sermonizing) love and liberation must come together—and that happens best, and deepest, through story and song. Milkman triumphs over everything, including himself. That is why the ambiguity of the novel's concluding lines is simultaneously appropriate and beside the point. Like the novel per se—and the magical realism which gives it its peculiar force—Milkman's final vision is an astonishing achievement, one that may begin in surprise, but that ends by convincing us that the imagination *is* transcendent, that, in ways mere realism could never understand, "if you surrendered to the air, you could *ride* it."

Notes

[1] *Roots* (Garden City, NY: Doubleday, 1976) 1. Subsequent references to the book appear parenthetically in the text.

[2] *What Was Literature?* (New York: Simon & Schuster, 1982) 228. Subsequent references to Professor Fielder are to this work; pagination is given parenthetically.

[3] For a fuller discussion of this phenomenon and its history, see the "Introduction" to Tom Wolfe's anthology *The New Journalism* (New York: Harper & Row, 1973).

[4] *Song of Solomon* (New York: Knopf, 1977) 3. Subsequent references to the novel appear parenthetically in the text.

[5] See Kathy Neustadt, "Two Major Events of the Year: The Visits of Writers Toni Morrison and Eudora Welty," *Bryn Mawr Alumnae Bulletin* Spring 1980: 5.

[6] "Black Family Chronicle," The New York *Times Book Review*, 11 September 1977: 48.

Reading Malamud's *The Tenants*, After a Quarter-Century of Black-Jewish Troubles

One of my favorite *New Yorker* cartoons is set on a university campus. All the requisite brush strokes are there: students strolling tree-lined campus walkways, bicycle racks, ivy-covered buildings. As a pair of academic statesmen descend the stairs, they notice two of their colleagues rolling around on the grass. Unlike them, these are longhaired, bearded types and this is fisticuffs of a high, if comically inept order. The caption reads: "I said right from the beginning, if you'll recall, that *two* poets-in-residence would never work out."

Not surprisingly, perhaps, that cartoon made an odyssey from a temporary, scotch-taped visit on my office door to more permanent digs above my writing desk. Among other things, the specter of writers duking it out serves to remind me that people with talent and aesthetic sensitivity can also be nasty, brutish, and mighty short on common sense. For most people, competition matters because one's success is measured by the bottom line, but there are places—academe is one of them—where ego counts for even more.

So, when I began to think about Malamud's *The Tenants*—first, for a class in Jewish-American literature and then for this occasion—how could this tale of two embattled writers *not* be somehow reflected through the prism of the cartoon staring back at me as I write these paragraphs? Granted, Malamud's exercise in imagining writerly blacks and Jews is hardly set on a cushy campus where words like "privilege" are much bandied about, but where real privilege turns out to be reduced teaching schedules, research assistants, reserved parking spots, and—dare I say it?—the chance to participate in panels like this one? Rather, he places Harry Lesser, his writerly Jew, in an apartment building that, like Lesser himself, has seen better days. Lesser's very name is a directional arrow of his writerly curve, one that threatens to go from *lesser* to "least." His third book, now some ten years in the *un*making, may have started its life in the temple of Lesser's Art, but now it quite literally stands for Lesser's life. Both are on the line, and as it were, in doubt.

For Levenspiel, the building's owner and the novel's one-man Greek chorus, the rickety steps and faulty plumping, the erratic furnace and broken windows, represent an opportunity—that is, if only the fiercely stubborn Lesser would accept his generous offers to relocate and make it possible for a new, more profitable apartment building to rise, phoenix-like, from the ashes of the old. After all, Lesser is not the only man lugging his bundle of griefs through the world. He, Levenspiel, has tsoris too: a crazy mother, a sick wife and a knocked-up teenaged daughter. Not surprisingly, Lesser won't budge because the building, wretched though it may be, has become his triggering town, his sorrow-riddled doppelganger. As he puts it: "Home is where my book is."

Enter Willie Spearmint, a young black writer who stakes out a squatter's spot in Lesser's building. The Morris dance that results, as each writer becomes simultaneously the other—and the Other—is what Malamud's dark fable of deteriorating black-Jewish relations means to explore. The result is a portrait of the Jewish writer as man of craft, consciousness, and extraordinary commitment. That said in admiration, what one must quickly add are the costs of such fussiness, for Lesser is also a man who labors on a novel about love with only the barest inkling of what the emotion is, or how wide its sacrifices are.

By contrast, Spearmint is meant to stand for black rage, in all its raw power, and aesthetic innocence. Each could, of course, learn from the other, but that is simply to remind us of the Yiddish maxim that you could live if they'd let you. The point is, you can't live, and Lesser-Spearmint don't learn. Granted, there are moments—lovely in their lyric power—when the struggle to turn their respective visions into Art transcends racial and ethnic barriers, but American literature is filled with similar instances, where the wheels fall off a utopian wagon. Consider, for example, *Adventures of Huckleberry Finn*. At the end of Twain's great novel, Huck's wonderfully vernacular voice explains how it is that Tom Sawyer got wounded: "He had a dream," Huck explains, "and it shot him." One could say much the same thing of the idyll on the raft that brought Huck to the shocking, then genuinely subversive conclusion that Nigger Jim is a man and not so much property to be bought and sold at an owner's whim. Rereading *The Tenants,* I was struck once again by our national dream of racial harmony, and by everything that militates against it. For Joyce's Stephen Dedalus, Ireland's tragic history as a land doubly oppressed by the British Crown and the Catholic Church constitutes the nightmare from which he cannot awaken; for American blacks and Jews, history is the wide gap between democratic promise and deep pockets of prejudice.

In an early Malamud story such as "Angel Levine," the dream was a good deal less complicated: blacks, as he proposed then, were really Jews under their pigmented skin—largely because everyone who suffers is, at bottom, a Jew. Sadly enough, recent history has disabused many of this notion, much as Twain's novel forced us to watch as Huck and Jim go their separate ways and the dream itself stares at you wielding a gun. I will argue that Malamud was prophetically aware of these possibilities nearly a quarter of a century ago, despite his insistence that the violent ending toward which Lesser and Spearmint move was a fantasy, and that only "mercy"—a word Levenspiel repeats 100+ times in the novel's final litany—can avert the severe decree.

Perhaps, but what we *see,* what we *feel* is the tragic inevitability of each writer murdering the other: Lesser by driving an ax through Spearmint's skull; Spearmint by aiming his razor at Lesser's genitals. If tragedy is the recognition that that which cannot be, must be; and that which must be, cannot be, then *The Tenants* is orchestrated—perhaps *over*orchestrated—to make its tragic point. In effect, Malamud manipulates stereotypes and arranges the rhythms of sadomasochism to create a scenario in which black rage meets Jewish restraint.

Jewish characters with a seemingly endless capacity for suffering had for so long been a Malamud trademark that nobody was especially surprised by a Lesser who earnestly, rhapsodically, sacrifices for his Art:

> He ran with his milk, bread, fruit, up six flights, chewing a cold apple. The small green automatic elevator, built for four, had expired not long ago. The attorney at the rent office had said the landlord must keep up essential services till Lesser moved out or they would order a reduction of his rent, but since he was screwing Levenspiel by staying on, keeping him from tearing down his building, out of mercy Lesser did not complain.

Militantly black characters are, of course, another matter,

and with Willie Spearmint, Malamud took an enormous risk. Etch them in exaggeration and charges of misrepresentation are sure to follow; romanticize them and face equally strong accusations of paternalistic condescension. As Spearmint puts it to Lesser during their first encounter: "I hate all that shit when whites tell you about black." The suspicions only deepen as Willie Spearmint transmogrifies himself into Bill Spear, the voice of black rage circa 1970, and as he moves inexorably toward a particularly chilling piece entitled "The First Pogram in the U.S. of A." As the white heat of Spearmint's racially charged imagination would have it, a group of ghetto guerrillas attempt to further the cause of Revolution by showing that a pogram can happen in America. They barricade a business block in Harlem and systematically work their way through its stores by shooting every Jew on their list. Lest there be any doubt about his bloody intentions, Spearmint pencils the following note on the last page of his story:

> It isn't that I hate the Jews. But if I do any, it's not because I invented it myself, but I was born in the good old U.S. of A. and there's a lot of that going on that gets under your skin. And it's also from knowing the Jews, which I do. The way to black freedom is against them.

Many of Malamud's liberal critics were at a loss to explain, much less to defend, his portrait of a black anti-Semite. Instead, they insisted that when Spearmint declares that "*I* am art. Willie Spearmint, *black man*. My form is *myself*," what we are getting is ugly parody rather than an accurate reflection of the black aesthetic movement. It would, of course, be pretty to think so, but the record of those times, those places, indicates otherwise. What I have in mind are such nearly-forgotten anthologies as William H. Grier and Price M. Cobb's *Black Rage* (1968), LeRoi Jones and Larry Neal's *Black Fire* (1968) or Addison Gayle, Jr.'s *Black Expression* (1969)—all published at a time when black undergraduates sported Afros, clenched fists, and insisted that Black Studies Programs (with appropriately separatist professors) be established immediately. Rage was the era's charged word, and if the arguments mounted on behalf of a black aesthetic movement sound familiar, it is because its angry words have simply been dusted off a quarter century later and offered up in the mouths of demagogues such as Professors Leonard Jeffries and Tony Martin, Ministers Louis Farrakahn and Kalid Muhammed. Here, for example, is James T. Stewart, from an essay entitled "The Development of the Black Revolutionary Artist" (1963):

". . . we must emancipate our minds from Western values and standards. We must rid our minds of these values. Saying so will not be enough"; and here is Hoyt W. Fuller, from "Towards a Black Aesthetic":

> . . . the break between the revolutionary black writers and the "literary mainstream" is, perhaps of necessity, cleaner and more decisive than the noisier and more dramatic break between the black militants and the traditional political and institutional structures. Just as black intellectuals have rejected the NAACP on the one hand, and the two major political parties, on the other, and gone off in search of new and more effective means and methods of seizing power, so revolutionary black writers have turned their backs on the old "certainties" and struck out in new, if uncharted, directions. They have begun the journey toward a black aesthetic. (1964)

All this, of course, has a deeply American ring (however incongruous the observation, then and now, might seem), for nothing so characterizes our cultural history as an insistence on the New and Improved. Unfortunately, the black aesthetic movement largely defined itself in terms of opposition, by what it was *not* rather than by what it was. The result is that one reads manifesto after strident manifesto from the architects of the black aesthetic movement only to discover that writers are valued in direct proposition to their non-Western, non-mainstream, and all too often, their anti-Semitic attributes. What such work expresses, however, often seems little more than its own inchoate rage. In this sense, the following lines—from LeRoi Jones's "Black Art"—are representative:

> . . . We want poems
> like fists beating niggers out of Jocks
> of dagger poems in the slimy bellies
> of the owner-Jews. . . .
> We want a black poem. And a
> Black World.
> Let the world be a Black Poem
> And Let All Black People Speak This Poem
> Silently or LOUD

Small wonder that the first incarnations of the black aesthetic movement fizzled; the marvel is that it should now have a new lease on life in writers who can once again capitalize on the reciprocal relationship between black rage and white guilt. Malamud was not alone in grieving about the dangers inherent in using Art to further bloodthirsty agendas; in their own ways,

Ralph Ellison and Irving Howe were equally alarmed. But the juggernaut had a noisy force of its own, and most white critics preferred to toe the party line rather than risk the ignominy of being written off as racists.

Little has changed. The black rage and black anti-Semitism Malamud courageously explored in *The Tenants* now threatens to join cries about "Wolf!" and "The Sky's Falling!" as phrases so overused that they lose their original force. As Stanley Crouch points out, in an important 1988 essay entitled "The Rage of Race," we should not be particularly surprised, for rage is the province of a people who have been "led up paths that resulted in imprisonment, spiritual collapse, and death for goals far less logical than acquiring political power through inclusion into the social contract."

Crouch, who clearly has as little sympathy for black nationalist postures as he does for white critics intimidated by them, brings a sense of history and a healthy streak of maverick independence to the essays collected as *Notes of a Hanging Judge* (1990). He understands, as Malamud, Howe, and Ellison did in the days when the black aesthetic movement first reared it head, that the Muse is a stubborn taskmaster and that Art requires more, much more, than rage. And no doubt he too would count himself with these earlier giants as one who believes in the unity of experience and culture; in the proposition that works of literature produced by blacks should be judged by the same aesthetic criteria as those produced by whites; and perhaps most of all, in a steadfast resistance to attempts to reestablish new versions of social and cultural segregation.

Unfortunately, Malamud, Ellison, and Howe are no longer with us, and Crouch's voice needs to be multiplied many fold. Otherwise, we are destined to suffer through Black Rage, Act II, with poems and essays as simple-minded, and dangerous, as those that clogged the book stores during ages that seem, at once, long ago and just like yesterday.

The Black Intellectuals' Common Fate and Uncommon Problems

> The people who come to evening classes are only ostensibly after culture. Their great need, their hunger, is for good sense, clarity, truth—even an atom of it. People are dying—it is no metaphor—for lack of something to carry home when day is done.
>
> —Moses Herzog

I

Among other things, Saul Bellow's *Herzog* (1964) is a portrait of the intellectual as a middle-aged man under great emotional stress. His "mental letters"—some feverishly jotted down, some simply imagined—tell us much about the immigrant ambitions that brought the New York intellectuals to national prominence, but perhaps even more about the limitations of intellectualism itself. For as Bellow makes clear in his introduction to Allan Bloom's *The Closing of the American Mind,* he wrote *Herzog* to show, among other things,

> how little strength "higher education" had to offer a troubled man. In the end he is aware that he has had no education in the conduct of life (at the university who was there to teach him how to deal with his erotic needs, with women, with family matters?) and he returns, in the language of games, to square one—or as I put it to myself while writing the book, to some primal point of balance.

Nonetheless, not *all* of Herzog's efforts end in narcissistic confusion, and with the quotation I have chosen as this essay's epigraph I mean to focus on the role that intellectuals can—indeed, *must*—play in a public world "dying" for even an atom of anything that smacks of good sense, clarity, and truth. Night school classes are, believe me, only one very small instance among thousands of others where even a glimmer of real understanding might make a difference. And nowhere is this truer than in the highly charged, intellectually perplexing topic of race.

Slightly more than 150 years ago, a man in his midthirties addressed initiates to Harvard's Phi Beta Kappa with words that were meant to open drowsy eyes, stir souls, and define the essential character of the American intellectual. Man, he argued—using the term generically, I might add—has become a fragmented creature, one defined by what he "does" rather than by what he *is*. Thus, "the planter, who is Man sent into the field to gather food, is seldom cheered by any idea of the truth of his ministry. He sees his bushel and his cart, and nothing beyond, and sinks into the farmer, instead of Man on the farm." Similar conditions apply to others circumscribed by their respective vocations: "The priest becomes a form; the attorney a statute-book; the mechanic a machine; the sailor a rope of the ship"; and most significant of all, the scholar, instead of *Man Thinking*, becomes "a mere thinker, or still worse, the parrot of other men's thinking."

By now most readers will recognize that the words I've been quoting belong to Ralph Waldo Emerson, and that they were taken from his justly famous essay "The American Scholar." But merely to catch the allusion is hardly sufficient, for what Emerson meant to sound that morning in Cambridge, Massachusetts, so many years ago was nothing less than America's *cultural* Declaration of Independence and, I would argue, the best definition of the intellectual's place in national affairs we have yet constructed.

Granted, we no longer share Emerson's buoyant, altogether confident optimism. He believed with every fiber of his being that a heroic American age beckoned just around his 19th-century corner—that is, once his fellow citizens rightly understood that the answer was *nature*. For Emerson, the term had wide transcendental orbits, but, taken together, what it implied was nothing less than the gravitational field that defined the American experience itself. Small wonder, then, that he kept repeating the word, insisting on its power in much the same way that his mantra of *soul, soul, and yet more soul* was meant to be a solution for normative religion's malaise. No doubt Emerson meant to pack worlds (possibly *too* many worlds) into his insistence on the centrality of American nature, but at least part of his program was to make it substitute for what passed in Europe as a cultural heritage. Given his observation that "we have listened too long to the muses of Europe"—or, in the current parlance, that we have overprivileged the Eurocentric—his emphases on self-reliance and originality are hardly surprising. "The sun shines today also," he declares in the first paragraph of *Nature*, a book that doubled as personal manifesto and cultural blueprint. "There is more wool and flax in the fields. There are new lands, new men, new thoughts. Let us demand our own works and laws and worship." Indeed, what he simultaneously demanded and prophetically called into existence was nothing more nor less than a distinctly American mode of thought.

Emerson, of course, had no monopoly on arguments premised on promises of the "new and improved." As a people, Americans have a long history of being suspicious of History. We swoon to the language of national specialness, to visions of America as a charmed place where the capacity to dream and the power to actualize is virtually identical. Emerson could tap into this abiding spirit at the same time he turned it inward, for what transcendentalism meant to unleash was the possibility of a society populated by imperial selves. Emerson's Concord neighbors were skeptical, and given the eccentricities of Thoreau or Margaret Fuller one can understand why. We need not, however, construct a complicated argument by way of "bottoms-up" history to appreciate just how difficult the delicate balancing of the competing claims by Self and Society could be for those lacking Emersonian conviction.

One of those simultaneously attracted and repelled by large transcendental promises was Nathaniel Hawthorne. In an age when American intellectuals strutted their stuff, he injected a quiet, cautionary note, usually by qualifying *nature* with the adjectival phrase, "man's sinful." Something about the very ease with which Emerson collected heroic souls (everyone from Napolean and Goethe to the mystically vaporous Swedenborg) led Hawthorne to self-doubt rather than giddy liberation. As Miles Coverdale, his thinly disguised surrogate in *The Blithedale Romance*, puts it: "The greatest obstacle to being heroic, is the doubt whether one may not be going to prove one's self a fool; the truest heroism is, to resist the doubt—and the profoundest wisdom, is to know when it ought to be resisted, and when to be obeyed." Given our current *Kulturkamf*, where words such as "Eurocentric" and "Afrocentric," "multiculturalism" and "diversity," are bandied about so loosely and often so irresponsibly that they carry more meaning as fighting words than as terms in a serious debate, Hawthorne's "test" for intellectual courage remains a good one. For in a world where Professor Leonard Jeffries spouts racist nonsense about the mystical properties of melanin or glibly divides the world into sun people and ice persons, where students increasingly demand that university curricula credential their respective identities and thus make them "feel good about themselves," it is hardly surprising that many academics find themselves wondering if discretion (read: silence) might not be the better part of valor. By contrast, intellectuals seek out the wisdom that distinguishes the martyr from the fool, the person who ought to stand tall from the one well advised to sit this one out. Because the widening racial divide is—one could argue, *always was*—our central national problem, I would argue that intellectuals have little choice, but I would also hasten to add that black intellectuals have both a special responsibility and a special burden—for their words cannot avoid raising suspicions just as they cannot avoid provoking consequences.

II

Thus was it ever as the American "experiment" set about to reconcile the idea with the reality, the noble words of our Founding Fathers with the deep divisions among its citizenry. More than a hundred years ago, Henry James, reflecting on the cultural conditions that severely delimited even so great an imaginative writer as Nathaniel Hawthorne, argued that the Civil War would sound an end to the nation's simplistic, uncritical faith that "there were no difficulties in the programme, no looming implications, no rocks ahead." At stake was nothing less than the loss of a collective innocence, and its replacement by what James felt would be a decidedly new American type:

> [The Civil War] introduced into the national consciousness a certain sense of proportion and relation, of the world being a more complicated place than it had hitherto seemed, the future more treacherous, success more difficult. . . . The good American, in days to come, will be a more critical person than his complacent and confident grandfather.

During the Reagan-Bush years one could rightly have doubts, for Americans—then and now—much prefer to hear about the "shining cittie on a hille" that was our first, and perhaps deepest, American Dream, and not about the worms of intolerance already squirming into John Winthrop's words as he uttered them aboard the *Arabella*. All of which is simply to point out that America cheers its boosters and gives its knockers the fish eye. Terms such as "criticism" or "critical detachment" lack the bracing power, the sheer *grip*, that certain ideas—manifest destiny, for example—still exert.

Nonetheless, James's "more critical person" is in most important respects akin to the energetic band of intellectuals who came to dominate the middle decades of this century, but whose continuing health and lively presence are now matters of some debate. We can see hints of the phenomenon in the special case of Henry Adams, a man who dabbled—sometimes impressively—in a wide range of disciplines (history, biography, anthropology, the natural sciences, medieval scholarship, painting, sculpture), but always as a self-professed, and usually self-deprecatory—"amateur."

Adams's aristocratic lineage may have included two U. S. presidents, but he himself lived in a post-Jacksonian age, forever excluded—or so he imagined—from the centers of public power. Nonetheless, power remained his abiding concern. His curiously modern, curiously *anti*-autobiography, *The Education of Henry Adams*, is, among other things, a continuing meditation about the impossibility of acquiring an adequate education at Harvard or, indeed, anywhere else. No doubt Adams would have taken a lively interest in our current squabbles about the canon, at least as they pit competing definitions of "education" against those that add up to a *mis*education; but I suspect he would also have noted that there is plenty of miseducation on both sides of the cultural divide. I say this because Adams's lot was to live in, and among, uncertainties. He may have taken his characteristic pose from an Enlightenment's conception of the man of letters, the *philosophe* in the mold of Voltaire and Diderot, yet everything about this oddly disappointed man points toward modernism.

Perhaps the best instance of Adams's predilection toward ironic ambivalence can be found in the single chapter of *The Education of Henry Adams* that stands as an emblem of his thought in roughly the same way that Jonathan Edwards's "Sinners in the Hands of an Angry God" has come to exemplify the shape-and-form of the Puritan sermon. That chapter, as those schooled in the Norton anthology already know, is "The Dynamo and the Virgin," an argument set in the great hall of the 1900

Paris Exposition as Adams desperately tries to come to grips with the new forms of energy, of power, of history itself, that the 20th century promises to unleash. Adams chooses to call his rumination of these competing forces "The Dynamo and the Virgin" because he means to contrast the energy that created the great cathedral at Chartres with the electrical current produced by 40-foot dynamos. Puritan America, Adams insists, could never understand the Virgin's power because Americans, then and now, think of sex as sinful rather than as fecund. By contrast, the dynamo, the machine, is an acceptable replacement both as symbol and as icon—for industrial power thrills us with promises of the every-Bigger, the ever-Faster, and, as our century discovered, the ever more Deadly.

That much said, let me hasten to add that Adams is a subtle thinker and those who would pluck the heart out of his arguments do so at their peril; but one thing is clear: Adams may well be the first in a long string of testy, alienated intellectuals who have made it their business to comment on the "commonweal" of the commonwealth. Granted, nothing about Adams himself—not his pedigrees, his wealth and social snobbery, or his social connections and Harvard crimson—would have endeared him to the radically independent group that formed around the *Partisan Review* and came to be known as the New York Intellectuals. They were, by contrast, a feisty plebian bunch, out to impose (or perhaps superimpose) a European model of culture onto America's native ground. On one essential matter, however, they would have made common cause with Adams, and that is the definition of an intellectual as one who specializes in being a nonspecialist. In many cases—one thinks of an Edmund Wilson or a Mary McCarthy—their writings covered not only a wide range of cultural subjects, but also a considerable gamut of creative genres. But what distinguishes these writers and made us regard them as literati in the best sense of the term were their contributions to belle-lettres, and especially to the literary essay as a mode of engagement with a culture's sense of itself.

William Phillips's playful quip that an intellectual was somebody who wrote for, or at least regularly read, the *Partisan Review* may be an exaggeration, but as one of the magazine's founding editors (along with Philip Rahv), he was in a position to gauge just how his pages differed from those of stuffier, more scholarly journals dedicated to German philology and what can now only be called the Very Old Criticism. What the New York intellectuals stood for was, at one and the same time, an adversary position, a critical stance, and perhaps most of all, a distinctive style, one Irving Howe described as "a flair for polemic, a taste for the grand generalization, an impatience with what they regarded (often parochially) as parochial scholarship, an internationalist perspective, and a tacit belief in the unity—even if a unity beyond immediate reach—of intellectual work."

In short, the New York intellectuals flourished in an age when the literary essay, written in plain, often blunt, English, mattered, and when there was a giddy sense that important struggles were being waged on behalf of a politics of the Left and the art of the avant-garde. Merely to recite the names of those who could be encountered regularly in the pages of *Partisan Review, Politics, Kenyon, VQR,* and *Sewanee* during the 1940s and 1950s—writers such as Dwight Macdonald, Irving Howe, Alfred Kazin, John Crowe Ransom, Alan Tate, Robert Penn Warren, Harold Rosenberg, Daniel Bell, Lionel Trilling—is to realize how difficult it would be to come up with a similarly impressive list for the present.

But that said, let me hasten to add an important caveat—namely, that nostalgia can assume many insidious forms, and that one of the most persistent is the assumption of a Golden Age from which our culture has now fallen. As this scenario argues, often in jeremiads echoing the Biblical "There were giants in those days," intellectual life had an independence, a vibrancy, a sense of mission, that no longer prevails. Rather than the maverick intellectual, we have the academic games-person, the intellectual-as-tenured-professor. Such people, Russell Jacoby argues in *The Last Intellectuals,* "no longer need or want a large public" because for the new kids on the intellectual block, "campuses are their homes; colleagues their audience; monographs and specialized journals their media."

Granted, Jacoby is hardly alone in figuring that civilization as he has come to know it will end when Alfred Kazin's review-essays no longer appear in the *New York Review of Books.* Others gaze at the mind-numbing prose being churned out at our most prestigious universities and despair. Indeed, in the years since Jacoby sounded his 1987 alarm, one could argue things "intellectual" have steadily gotten worse. And while I would readily admit that examples of errant foolishness gussied up as intellectual thought are easy to collect (in truth, they always were), I would also argue that we need to resist the dubious attractions of a then-good/bad-now syndrome. For the truth is that the same squabbles about canonicity and multiculturalism that produce sound bites on "Nightline" and "The MacNeil-Lehrer Hour" or that have turned debates about political correctness into a cash cow for print journalism have also prompted important redefinitions of intellectual work.

In this regard, the New York intellectuals have proven themselves a livelier, more resilient bunch than the prophets of doom predicted, for if anti-Stalinism no longer occupies the central position it once did, there are no shortages of cultural threats serious enough to cause what remains of the old crowd, and some newer members, to rally once again around their typewriters. The results are regular installments from the likes of Cynthia Ozick and Leon Wieseltier, Robert Alter and Leonard Kriegel, about what it means to be a public intellectual at a time when the culture itself is going through a bad, often infuriating patch. Indeed, the sheer volume of nonsense written by those with a head for social constructions of reality has been a boon for public intellectuals of the old school, for while the former have pinned their academic hopes on a dizzying array of "theories" (everything from deconstruction to the New Historicism), the latter have kept faith with words like "individual" and paragraphs unafraid to use an "I."

One could argue, of course, that there is precious little new here, that public intellectuals have *always* imagined themselves as bucking whatever tide seems currently fashionable. The trick has always been to be "critical" in opposing the social mainstream and yet "cultural" in speaking for that mainstream. Often this meant balancing blessings with curses, large promises with ignoble realities, and perhaps most of all, an impulse to boost against an obligation to knock. Thus, as a consensus began to emerge—say, around politically loaded terms such as "diversity" or "inclusion"—many of the latter-day New York intellectuals raised hard questions, and when the occasion warranted, vigorous dissent.

Skepticism, in short, continues to come with their territory, along with generous doses of irony (including its self-lacerating versions) and not a little of the sarcasm for which they were once justly famous. Granted, some New York intellectuals specialized in irony, others in withering sarcasm, but what they "shared" was an isolation, a loneliness, that may well be the intellectual's common fate. That my last sentence surrounds *shared* with inverted commas is deliberate, at once a way of describing a group that made much, perhaps too much, of their alienation and at the same time, suggesting that they "shared" this conviction in roughly the same manner as everything else—namely, with skepticism, irony, and sarcasm. Here, a story told about the late Irving Howe is instructive. When an ambitious young scholar asked him if he would agree that mutual support, in a word, "back-scratching," had a good deal to do with the phenomenal success of certain New York intellectuals, Howe offered this not-so-friendly amendment: "If you changed 'back' to 'eye' you might have something."

Not since Emerson (a figure most New York intellectuals regarded with deep suspicion) has there been a greater concentration of people whose sense of self seemed so directly proportional to their capacity for being misunderstood—by kindred thinkers, the general public, and, of course, their fellow Jews. Literary histories of that time, that place, differ about emphasis and interpretation (e.g., Was Trilling an old-line liberal, a crypto-neoconservative, or none of the above?), but on one matter there is general agreement—namely, that the New York intellectuals were a testy, combative bunch.

That their polemical inclinations made for brilliant essays and memorable quips is true enough, but it is also worth pointing out that these came at a certain human cost. Again, Howe may have said it best when, in the late 1960s, he found himself accused of success—defined, of course, as "selling out"—by those on the New Left:

> But really, when you come to think of it, what did this "success" of the intellectuals amount to? A decent or a good job, a chance to earn extra money by working hard, and in the case of a few, like Trilling and Kazin, some fame beyond New York—rewards most European intellectuals would take for granted, so paltry would they seem. . . . What the "leftist" prigs of the sixties failed to understand—or perhaps understood only too well—was that the "success" with which they kept scaring themselves was simply one of the possibilities of adult life, a possibility, like failure, heavy with moral risks and disappointment. The whole business: debts, overwork, vericose veins, alimony, drinking, quarrels, hemorrhoids, depletion, the recognition that one might not prove to be another T. S. Eliot, but also some good things, some lessons learned, some "rags of time" salvaged and precious.

Put a slightly different way, poverty will always seem romantic to people who imagine it from the perspective of lives formed by suburban affluence. Thus, one identified with "the people" by donning the hairshirt of the times—tie-dye for some, blue chambray for others—and insisting that "purity" be at once a litmus test and badge of honor. Not surprisingly, the result was an ugly standoff, with radical activists manning the barricades on one side and older-fashioned intellectuals shaking their heads on the other.

What I've been describing, of course, played itself out against the backdrop of a war that raised hard questions about intellectual life in America, and that ultimately divided those who cheered when *The New York Review of Books* displayed a molotov cocktail and those who stared at it with pinched faces. In this regard, the title of Norman Podhoretz's 1979 book—*Breaking Ranks*—may have said all that is necessary about why some New York intellectuals took an abrupt turn to the Right, and why even those who did not officially join the exodus could not, in good conscience, support much that they saw on the cultural horizon.

III

Enter the new generation of black intellectuals—everyone from Henry Louis Gates, Jr., Stephen Carter, and Cornel West to Shelby Steele, Orlando Patterson and Stanley Crouch. Taken together, they represent a direction that began 40 years ago with the *Brown vs. Board of Education* decision and continued through the civil rights movement. In short, the black intellectual voices now speaking out from our most prestigious universities are, as the title of Stephen Carter's 1991 book would have it, "affirmative action babies." From token representation in the 1950s and 60s—when, say, Harvard typically admitted ten blacks per class—enrollments have fairly soared as Afro-American studies programs took root (often in response to student protest) and universities slowly but surely embraced a new educational paradigm based on race, class, and gender.

In the process, culture became, well, one of those words. It was once spelt with a capital letter, defined by Matthew Arnold as "the best that has been thought and said," and generally agreed to be a good thing. Now, many in the academy were not so sure, partly because selecting the "best" invariably means leaving out the "least," and partly because culture itself often seems to be a suspect operation. Rather than "sweetness and light" (the title of the Arnold essay in which his famous definition appeared), "culture"—yet another term destined to be surrounded by inverted commas—stands for everything that first bullies and then silences minority voices.

No one would seriously argue with the proposition that black intellectuals have played a major role in the culture wars that define our time. Indeed, some would insist that they are what the New York intellectuals once were—namely, activist scholars who bring fresh blood and new perspectives to our understanding of American culture. At the same time, however, there are important differences. Regardless of how much the New York intellectuals were divided by temperament and later, by politics, they shared a fund of common experience that, for want of a better term, might be called "immigrant gratitude." America, and perhaps more to the point, American culture, offered an escape from the hardships and parochial limitations that had narrowly defined the lives of their immigrant parents. Granted, the giddy possibility of self-transformation did not come without cost, and it would take a long arc indeed before many would rediscover the Jewishness from which they had fled. Not surprisingly, the conflict was the very stuff of which intellectuals, rather than scholars, are made, for as Daniel Bell once shrewdly observed, the scholar finds his place within an established tradition and adds his tiny piece to the mosaic. By contrast, the intellectual begins with "HIS experiences, HIS individual perceptions of the world, HIS privileges and deprivations, and judges the world by these sensibilities."

Bell had the New York intellectuals in mind as he fashioned his distinction, but the terms apply with equal force to black public intellectuals, including those with Ivy League pedigrees and solidly academic books. Indeed, with the notable exception of Stanley Crouch, a fiercely independent, no-nonsense type, the most promising black intellectuals are the creations of and by academia. But that said, let me hasten to add that, with minor adjustments, much the same thing could be said of the W. E. B. DuBois who was a product of Harvard and Heidelberg every bit as much as he was formed by the "color line" he regarded as the central problem of our century.

Indeed, I would argue that it is important to resist both the impulse to romanticize, and thus overpraise, the effort of autodidacts such as James Baldwin or Ralph Ellison as well as the equally naïve inclination to undervalue the impressive accomplishments of Henry Louis Gates, Jr. or Cornel West. After all, what made Baldwin and Ellison important writers then is precisely what makes Gates and West noteworthy cultural figures now—namely, the accretion of ideas and influences, a "sorting out" that leads to an individual voice, and finally, most importantly, the use to which these disparate elements are put. To ask that young black intellectuals rekindle the spirit that led to the Harlem Renaissance in the 1920s or, for that matter, to the heyday of the New York intellectuals in the 1940s and 1950s is to ignore the handwriting on the university wall. Rather than reading "Abandon hope all ye of dark skin who enter here"—as the unwritten signs once did—the message blaring out of our colleges and universities today is *Welcome, welcome*. What one should rightly ask, then, is where, and for what, do they stand as public intellectuals?

At this point, the answer will not only depend upon which figures pop up on your mental screen—Henry Louis Gates, Jr. or Houston Baker? Cornel West or Leonard Jeffries? Shelby Steele or Molefi K. Asante?—but also on what you imagine as the proper role for intellectuals, black and white, at a time when race threatens to once again divide our nation into warring camps. Thus far I have stressed elements of the black intellectuals' common fate without directly addressing the devil that always lurks in the details. So, let me now say it more bluntly: the very qualities that define an intellectual are precisely those that effective leaders learn to suppress, for if the former are defined by their capacity to maintain a certain critical distance; to value complexity, not for its own sake, but because a genuine consideration of the issues demands it; and perhaps above all, to never flinch in the face of controversy, all too often the latter are studies in savvy calculation, accomplished deception, and perfect opacity. Leaders, in a word, know what *works*, and they make certain that their "messages" are simultaneously simple and aimed at a single purpose. Small wonder, then, that W. E. B. DuBois's conflict with Booker T. Washington was an accident waiting to happen, or that the first, and possibly greatest, black intellectual later found himself at odds with the NAACP, the very organization he helped bring into being.

To be sure, many intellectuals find ways to combine cultural criticism with activist politics. One thinks, for example, of

Philip Rahv, of Irving Howe, of DuBois himself. But the present moment has raised the ante and altered the ground rules, especially for those black intellectuals unwilling to toe the separatist line that dismisses integration as a dream gone sour. Nor is there much solace in remembering that Baldwin felt much the same sense of isolation, caught as he was between his large ambitions to be an American writer and the narrow confines of his skin, for the pain that follows each success of a Henry Louis Gates, Jr. or a Cornel West is of a radically different sort. For example, when Gates wrote what may be the central truth about our collective experience as black and white Americans—namely, that each is a product of the other's imagination—or when he warned against efforts to construct a monolithic version of what is, or is not, "black," the grumblings began in Harvard Yard and quickly rippled out to even angrier black constituencies who get their information from the *Amsterdam News*. Its response, by the way, was that Harvard had ruined more black folk than whiskey ever did. And when Gates used the pages of *The New York Times* to expose *The Secret Relationship Between Blacks and Jews*, a work that wraps its virulent anti-Semitism in the folds of footnotes and pseudo-scholarship, he received death threats.

But one need not point to sensational instances because the sad truth is we have become so accustomed to people cynically playing the race card that even black intellectuals must wonder if *anything* they write could have the galvanizing power, much less generate the same ink, as a single speech by the likes of a Leonard Jeffries. In this sense, black anti-Semitism is more symptom than cause, a way of directing rage against a group that stands, as it were, for a collective whiteness. Meanwhile, black life in America has become a pitched battle between the haves and have-nots, between those who refuse to write America down in a single word—*racist*—despite regular, galling reminders that skin color still matters mightily, and those who think that voluntary segregation is a notable improvement over the old, bad versions imposed by an old, bad South. No doubt when black intellectuals watch the evening news they must experience something of the same feeling Edmund Wilson had when he claimed that he did not recognize the America reflected in *Life* magazine. This is surely not what they had in mind when they embarked on their careers and found themselves surprised by the prestige and influence they earned. Indeed, they might respond by asking "What influence?" as if anything they write or speak could change the dailiness of daily life on the nation's meaner streets. As Cornel West puts it:

> The choice of becoming a black intellectual is an act of self-imposed marginality; it assures a peripheral status in and to the black community. The quest for literacy indeed is a fundamental theme in Afro-American history and a basic impulse in the black community. But for blacks, as with most Americans, the uses for literacy are usually perceived to be for some substantive pecuniary benefits rather than those of the writer, artist, teacher, or professor.

Defined this way, marginality is an intellectual's common fate, no different for Cornel West than it was for me. When my grandfather heard that I was headed for a graduate degree in English, he was shocked because so far as he was concerned I spoke "a gooteh Henglish" already. No doubt West's parents sounded their notes of bemusement in a different key, but the essential music remained the same. I suspect it always was.

Where the condition of black intellectuals differs, however, and where their problems strike me as "uncommon," is in the sense, both culturally created and self-induced, that race is the only subject worth writing about because it alone will generate readers. Who, after all, would be interested in what Henry Louis Gates, Jr. has to say about Herman Melville's white whale or Nathaniel Hawthorne's Puritan guilt, much less about the "manners" that energize the worlds of Jane Austen or George Eliot? Granted, Cornel West has a book about American pragmatism that grinds its way through Dewey, Mills, Pierce, Quine, and Rorty, but the book that sold, and sold BIG, was *Race Matters*. I say this not to suggest that black intellectuals should shy away from being what Gates calls "race men," committed to a literature of great beauty and power, but, rather, to raise a question that speaks to white readers as well as black writers.

To alter a memorable line from "The Godfather," with intellectuals it's never "business," but always *personal*. By that I mean, they bring large measures of themselves to whatever happens to spark their interest. Thus, when Irving Howe wrote about Hardy or about Faulkner, his thumbprint was plainly evident on every page. Indeed, how could it be otherwise, given that how he read was filtered through a sensibility formed in the crucible of immigrant Jewish life? Black intellectuals have similar opportunities, but, thus far, they seem exceptions rather than the rule. Consider, for example, the instructive differences between the Massey lectures Irving Howe delivered at Harvard, and that became *The American Newness,* a consideration of the Emersonian tradition in American letters that he had dismissed (perhaps too quickly) as a young man and later came to value, with the Massey lectures Toni Morrison's recently delivered as *Playing in the Dark.* One could argue that both efforts were efforts at "expansion," but where Howe imagines America, Morrison works to reify our definition. The differences are important, and they tell us much about how solidly the color line remains in place, both as a defining, and I would argue, limiting condition.

In Baldwin's "Notes of a Native Son," he confesses that "I have not written about being a Negro at such length because I expected that to be my only subject, but only because it was the gate I had to unlock before I could hope to write about anything else, " Forty years later, "Negro" has been replaced by black, and in some circles, by African-American, but for too many black intellectuals, the gate remains as unlocked as ever.

And this, as much as anything, is the uncommon problem that they must squarely face. One can, of course, point to the Ralph Ellison whose magisterial novel, *The Invisible Man,* is still the finest blending of black experience and Matthew Arnold's "best that has been thought and said" or to Gate's impressive disquisition on First Amendment squabbles in the pages of a recent *New Republic,* but I think that Stephen Carter's *The Culture of Disbelief,* a consideration of the ways religion has been elbowed out of our national discourse and the consequences of that dubious victory, is a more promising example. For the strength of Carter's arguments lies in the arguments themselves, rather than in the fact that he is black. Indeed, his blackness simply ceases to matter, in roughly the same way that what a person says should count for more than the skin or gender or whatever of the respective mouth.

Unfortunately, we have become so hyperconscious, so paralyzed, by race that I do not look forward to fundamental changes in attitude any time soon. Perhaps it is enough to applaud those black intellectuals willing to stand tall against the loopier versions of the new bigotry and to insist that Black Studies programs be something more than exercises in "feeling good." Those stands, modest and commonsensical as they might seem, have not been uttered without cost or without courage.

For to gain the approval of whites is to risk the approbation of many in the black community. And that too remains yet another instance of the "uncommon problems" that black intellectuals currently face. No doubt there are more, and I suspect we'll hear about them as black intellectuals discover that there is strength in numbers, albeit of a strained and complicated sort. And if this sounds remarkably like the condition of the New York intellectuals during their days of highest energy and maximum tension, so be it. For the "clarity, good sense, truth—even an atom" those intellectuals once provided has been sorely missed by exactly the sort of people who once crowded into Moses Herzog's evening classes. They are still out there, just as confused as ever about the bromides of editorials and the sound bites of ideologues. All of which is to suggest that the opportunities for black intellectuals have never been greater, nor has the need.

When Black/Jewish Relations Turned Sour, And Why

Broken Alliance: The Turbulent Times Between Blacks and Jews in America. By Jonathan Kaufman. New York: Charles Scribner's Sons, 1988. 311 pp. $19.95.

Broken Alliance began innocently enough—as an effort by a young reporter to explain the shouting match that followed a talk at the *Boston Globe* offices by Black Muslim minister Louis Farrakhan. Not that Farrakhan had anything new or particularly "newsworthy" to say. It was, Kaufman reports, the standard line, but the deep divisions it created afterward were emblematic of how far even professional newspaper writers had come since the halcyon days when "We Shall Overcome" was on lips black and white, and when Martin Luther King, Jr.'s "dream" created a special sense of secret sharing between blacks and Jews. Farrakhan's angry words made it clear that a great deal of troubled water had been collecting since King's tragic death:

How, black reporters asked, could Jews claim to be political allies but be so opposed to quotas and critical of affirmative action? How, Jewish reporters responded, could blacks be so blind to the impact of the Holocaust and brush off the terror Jews felt at any anti-Semitic slur, vulnerable in a world that could always turn hostile.

Kaufman, who was born two years after the landmark 1954 *Brown v. Board of Education* decision, grew up taking black-Jewish cooperation for granted. He knew that the first two presidents of the NAACP had been Jewish brothers (the Spingarns), that Jack Greenberg had headed the NAACP Legal Defense Fund, that Jews had been prominent contributors to the National Urban League, to CORE, to the Congress of Racial Equality, that Jews had marched in the Civil Rights Movements and that two of them—Michael Schwerner and Andrew

Goodman—had been martyred in the struggle.

Kaufman also knew that the psychic bonds that linked Jews to blacks and blacks to Jews were very deep. After all, had not James Baldwin written that "The Negro identifies himself almost wholly with the Jew. The more devout Negro considers that he is a Jew, in bondage to a hard taskmaster and waiting for a Moses to lead him out of Egypt"; and had not Kaufman grown up in a world where the annual ritual of the Passover seder made it palpably clear that we were once slaves, and, therefore, uniquely positioned to feel *rachmones*, and to cry out for justice, with regard to blacks?

In short, Kaufman found himself asking, what once brought blacks and Jews together, and what has wrenched them apart? *Broken Alliance* is his attempt to answer these complicated questions—not through encyclopedic, or even systematic, research; not by presenting a comprehensive history; not by imposing Large Ideas onto the present condition. Rather, Kaufman decided to tell what he found out "through a set of six seriel biographies—the stories of five individuals and one family (three black and three Jewish) whose lives reflected the ebbs and flows, the triumphs and losses of black-Jewish relations over the past thirty years. The result is a tapestry—an extremely readable one, I might add—that shows how a coalition came together, how it worked great change, and how it gradually fell apart. Granted, Kaufman's study *is* a highly selective one, and those out to quarrel with his conclusions need only point to the limitations of his "control group" as Exhibit A. But if his methodology is the stuff that *reportage*, rather than sociology, is made, his engaging portraits of Paul Parks and Jack Greenberg, Rhody McCoy and Bernie and Roz Ebstein, Martin Peretz and Donna Brazile remind us that human beings—rather than abstractions —are at the center of his story.

Unlike, say, the Quakers, American Jews did not have a history of becoming involved in liberal causes, even during the Civil War. This statement—which opens Kaufman's thumbnail sketch of Jewish life in America—will no doubt come as something of a surprise to those who equate Jewishness with liberal social attitudes. But the bald truth is that those Jews who came to America in the seventeenth, eighteenth, and early nineteenth centuries were heirs of a conservative political tradition, one that valued the status quo much more than it did efforts to rock the boat. America represented a land where they might be treated equally, where they might escape the sting of bigotry, where democracy promised what monarchs could arbitrarily withhold. Small wonder, then, that American Jews were as divided as the rest of America on the slavery issue: there were Jewish abolitionists and also Jewish slave-owners; and no doubt there were Jews whose opinions on the matter were precisely the same as their gentile neighbors. As Kaufman puts it, "Notwithstanding the prophetic tradition of the Old Testament prophets who inveighed against injustice, inequality, and poverty, the Jews who came to America before the Civil War harbored a deep-seated—and historically justified—uneasiness of mass protest movements. They were unwilling to defy the law of the land or cast their lot with poor, oppressed people who might easily one day turn their anger on the Jews."

The huge mave of Russian Jewish immigration not only changed the arithmetic (two million+ new arrivals between 1880 and 1920 versus the 250,000 Jews already here), but also altered prevailing social attitudes. Attuned to the currents of European socialism, burning with a variety of revolutionary fevers, the new immigrants had a keen sense both of what exploitation was and how collective action, solidarity, *brotherhood,* could combat it. Following the East St. Louis riot in 1917 in which thirty-nine blacks were killed, the *Jewish Daily Forward* compared the riot to the Kishinev pogram of 1903, when more than fifty Jews were killed: "Kishinev and St. Louis—the same soil, the same people."

But that said, Kaufman unrolls the highpoints of the "alliance" in ways that suggest where seeds of future discontent were sown. Unease existed on both sides, even as they met in cooperative efforts and affected important changes. If Jews could be counted on as friends—in greater numbers and with more staying power than virtually any other group—their assistance did not come without a certain cost. Jews were fearsome debaters, sharp lawyers, savvy tacticians. In a phrase, they gave every appearance of "taking over," and in ways that struck blacks as patronizing, as condescending, and often as both. If it is true that blacks admired Jews, it was also true that they resented them; conversely, if it is true that Jews felt a natural empathy for blacks, it is also true that they felt superior.

The words that spelled the difference, that brought these long-simmering resentments to rapid boil, were *Black power.* In what struck many Jews as a betrayal, longstanding allies in the good fight were suddenly disenfranchised by virtue of skin color alone. What had been the anthem of the Civil Rights Movement—"Black and white together/We shall overcome"—became a litany of separatist gestures and blatantly anti-Semitic attacks.

Kaufman's portraits serve to fill in the human faces of those who lined up on the side of Martin Luther King, Jr. and those who regarded him as so much "old news." In general, the breakup has mattered more to Jews than to blacks. Granted, there are some (Martin Peretz, for example) who have become so disillusioned with the prospects of black-Jewish relations that they cannot imagine the breach *ever* being repaired. Others have confidence that the day will yet return when blacks and Jews will do more than shout at each other over charges of racism, anti-Semitism, and deep political differences. History, after all, is a very old story and one could argue that the psychic resonances that blacks and Jews share still matter. But as Kaufman concludes, "if Jews often express a nostalgia for the alliance, or puzzlement that it were awry, blacks, by and large, do not." Meanwhile, the relative affluence of American Jews and the increasingly downward spiral of the black community make prospects for reconciliation more difficult, but paradoxically, more essential than ever.

The Content of Our Character: A New Vision of Race in America. By Shelby Steele. New York: St. Martin's Press, 1990. 175 pp. $15.95.

That a young black intellectual should write about race in America is hardly surprising; but if the book begins with an epigraph from Saul Bellow ("Of all that might be omitted in thinking, the worst was to omit your own being") and later quotes approvingly from Ralph Ellison's *Invisible Man*, it is likely to raise eyebrows. And if it goes on to provoke serious questions about the crippling effects of black entitlements (everything from affirmative-action programs to preferential college admissions), it will almost certainly produce howls of disapproval from those, white and black, who cling tenaciously to their respective scripts. But the very predictability of such responses is precisely Steele's point: "Race is an area in which Americans have been conditioned by a history of painful conflict into a rigid and unforgiving propriety. Each race has its politics and its party line that impose a certain totalitarianism over the maverick thoughts of the individual."

By contrast, Steele addresses the troubled racial climate of the 1990s in ways that drive deeper, and look further, than anything currently coming out of the NAACP or the White House. He does this not as a sociologist or political expert (Steele is, in fact, an English professor) but as somebody convinced that "*The most dangerous threat to the black identity is not the racism of white society (this actually confirms the black identity), but the black who insists on his or her own individuality.*" Small wonder, then, that Steele has such high praise for Ellison's *Invisible Man*, and especially for those lines which speak to personal responsibility: "Our task is that of making ourselves individuals. . . . We create the race by creating ourselves and then to our great astonishment we will have created something far more important: we will have created a culture."

The protagonist of Ellison's novel learns—in one painful

initiation after another—just how subtle, how insidious, the fashioners of his "invisibility" can be; and nearly forty years later, Steele finds himself warring against those who would turn the dubious advantages of victimhood into the New Invisibility. Often this means he must offer a wholesale dismissal of what has come to be known as the "black agenda":

> . . . that white racism and racial discrimination are still the primary black problems; that blacks should maintain an essentially adversarial stance toward the mainstream; that institutional racism is automatically present in the workplace; that political conservatism is by definition anti-black; that blacks are not "given" enough chances to advance; that blacks are exploited economically and otherwise because they are black; that the larger society is basically indifferent to the problem of blacks; that high black crime rates are the outgrowth of victimization; that blacks must work twice as hard to gain recognition as whites; that one should be black first and American second.

Steele freely admits that there are nuggets of truth in these assumptions (given our long, sad history of racial turmoil, how could there *not* be?), but their net effect is to undervalue the genuine accomplishments of the civil-rights movement and, more important, to "make the black identity an identity of accusation that offers its subscribers a way to recompose their vulnerability into their victimization." It also ensures that blacks will continue to be "innocent" and that whites will continue to be "guilty," and that both will remain invisible—to each other as well as to themselves.

Indeed, blacks have become so comfortable in their collective invisibility that Steele's call for "individual effort within the American mainstream" will no doubt strike many of them as just what might be expected from an author who rattles on about his integrated neighborhood, his two cars, and his white wife. And whites who prefer to see blacks as problems in social engineering (rather than as individuals) will find themselves equally uncomfortable when they are taken to task for smothering personal responsibility in the blanket of black entitlement. But Steele means to make genuine freedom and authentic selfhood the demanding, hard-won commodities they in fact are and must be. As he puts it on the final page of *The Content of Our Character*, "I believe it is time for blacks to begin to shift from a wartime to a peacetime identity, from fighting for opportunity to the seizing of it." Mass action may well have been necessary in the 1960s; in the 1990s, however, racial advancement can only come through "hard work, education, individual initiative, stable family life, property ownership." And Steele couches his no-nonsense message in a way that offers a challenge to and an indictment of the black middle class, one seldom seen—at least in public print:

> It has always annoyed me to hear from the mouths of certain arbiters of blackness that middle-class blacks should "reach back" and pull up those blacks less fortunate than they—as though middle-class status was an unearned and essentially passive condition in which one needed a large measure of noblesse oblige to occupy one's time. My own image is of reaching back from a moving train to lift on board those who have no tickets. A noble enough sentiment—but might it not be wiser to show them the entire structure of principles, effort, and sacrifice that puts one in a position to buy a ticket anytime one likes?

Steele's emphasis is on character rather than color, on the individual rather than the race. As his title suggests, he numbers himself among those who also dream of the day when, as Martin Luther King's "I Have a Dream" speech puts it, "children will be judged not by the color of their skin, but by the content of their character." This, despite the abundant evidence that the sayings of Malcolm X—and the black separatism they espouse—are more popular on inner-city streets and college campuses. Perhaps it was inevitable that the efforts on behalf of integration would lead first to the backlash of black power, then to our current bean-counting talk about numbers and racial balance. But as Steele reminds us, integration "once stood for a high and admirable set of values. It made a difference second to communality, and it asked members of all races to face whatever fears they inspired in each other." We have, to our discredit, chosen the easier paths of racial politics, with its power-broking of black victimization and its white "quick fixes." What we have *not* dared to do is move beyond the color line, where individuals become "visible" and where they are held accountable for their successes and failures.

Granted, Steele's "vision" is not an easy one. As he points out,

> Guilt is the essence of white anxiety just as inferiority is the essence of black anxiety. And the terror that it carries for whites is the terror of discovering that one has reason to feel guilt where blacks are concerned—not so much because of what blacks might think but because

> of what guilt can say about oneself. If the darkest fear of blacks is inferiority, the darkest fear of whites is that their better lot in life is at least partially the result of their capacity for evil—their capacity to dehumanize an entire people for their own benefit and then to be indifferent to the devastation their dehumanization has wrought on successive generations of their victims.

Wriggling out of this double bind will not—indeed, *cannot*—come without considerable psychic cost. But recognizing the problem is often the first step toward seeing the Other as one's human counterpart, and in this spirit let me simply admit that there are whole sections of Steele's book—particularly when he writes about racial turmoil on our nation's campuses—where I nod in agreement at the same time that I know full well I would have held back from writing his lines:

> How many black students demonstrating for black theme dorms—demonstrating in the style of the sixties, when the battle was to win for blacks a place on campus—might be better off spending their time reading and studying? Black students have the highest dropout rate and the lowest grade point average of any group in America. This need not be so. And it is not the result of not having black theme dorms.
>
> . . . .
>
> Black students have not sufficiently helped themselves, and universities, despite all their concessions, have not really done much for blacks. If both faced their anxieties, I think they would see the same thing: academic parity with all other groups should be the overriding mission of black students, and it should also be the first goal that universities have for their black students. Blacks can only *know* they are as good as others when they are, in fact, as good—when their grades are higher and their dropout rate lower. Nothing under the sun will substitute for this, and no amount of concessions will bring it about.

At other spots I find myself disputing Steele's argument. Sometimes I am bothered by his penchant for facile psychologizing (e.g., home-brewed concoctions like "*seeing for innocence*" or forays into "race-holding"). Elsewhere I protest his efforts to dismiss both the black underclass and history itself with the sweep of a well-groomed 1990 hand. As a Jew who has seen how delimiting some versions of "Jewish history" can be, I understand Steele's impatience with those who will explain every black problem, be it teen pregnancies or Mayor Marion Barry's arrest, as yet another manifestation of white racism. But when he likens memory to "the man who wears a heavy winter coat in springtime because he was frostbitten in winter," I think both his metaphor and its point badly misfire. I would argue instead that black history is, in a very real sense, *American* history, and that both whites and blacks need to confront our deeply troubled past if we are to have any hope of a less troubled future.

At one point in a discussion of our strong inclination to "deny and recompose," Steele suggests that all of us must monitor our impulses—and that "for this, we will need all the critical voices we can find." Steele's is such a voice, and after public discussion moves beyond whether he is or is not a neoconservative "entitlement basher," I suspect that *The Content of Our Character* will serve to sharpen debate for a very long time.

Singing the Blues
All the Way to the Bank

The Rage of a Privileged Class. By Ellis Cose. HarperCollins. $20.00.

That yet another book makes a case for how and why racism pulls at the national fabric is hardly news, but when its title purposefully cobbles "rage" with "privilege" and its author goes on to argue that behind the trappings of success—Ivy League educations, six-figure incomes, magisterial homes—middle-class blacks are both angry and disillusioned, what are those of us who had hoped for quite a different conclusion to do? For if the Civil Rights Movement is written off as a failure and the fruits of affirmative action programs are as bitter as Ellis Cose suggests, then the distinctions between the inner-cities and the suburbs no longer matter and we are in deeper trouble than even the likes of Andrew Hacker (*Two Nations*) or Studs Terkel (*Race*) had suspected when they published their studies of America's deteriorating racial climate only four short years ago. Granted, the case for hand-wringing despair is simultaneously as old as Alex De Tocqueville's *Democracy in America* (1865) and as recent as Derrick Bell's *Faces at the Bottom of the Well* (1992). Pessimism, in short, has its permanent attractions, not the least being that where racial matters are concerned, it seems always a safer bet. What Cose adds to the grim prophecies already in is a focus on those blacks who discovered rather late in the game that the usual yardsticks of the American dream—hard work and achievement, material success and psychic well-being—do not apply to them, because no matter how many prestigious degrees they collect or how large a salary they command, the indignities of second-class citizenship continue to sting. As Mayor David Dinkins put it, in words meant to echo Malcolm X's famous quip about black Ph.D.s, a black millionaire is finally nothing more than "a nigger with a million dollars." And as such, he can look forward to cabs whizzing past him on Manhattan streets or to the very real possibility of being rousted by the cops when he stops at a suburban Seven-Eleven for milk and eggs.

The Rage of a Privileged Class's provocative title is followed by two sub-titled questions: "Why Are Middle-Class Blacks Angry?" and "Why Should America Care?" The burden of his study, then, is first to explain the rage bubbling just beneath those putatively successful blacks who spend their lives staring upward at corporate glass ceilings, and then to budge white Americans from the denial best typified by Senator Daniel Patrick Moynihan's feeling that the black middle class was "moving along quite nicely" and that the big problem is "what are we going to do about the underclass?" My hunch is that a good many Americans, both white and black, share Moynihan's view that "rage" is more appropriate when applied to the meaner streets of South Central L.A. than it is to the manicured lawns of New Rochelle and that urban crime matters more than tears shed onto silken pillowcases.

Cose, I hasten to add, is well aware of the objections his thesis will raise, but he insists that the troubles of the black underclass do not—indeed, *must* not—cancel out the justifiable anger felt by those who have "moved on up," for

> . . . though the problems of the two classes are not altogether the same, they are in some respects linked. Moreover, one must at least consider the possibility that a nation which embitters those struggling hardest to believe in it and work within its established systems is seriously undermining any effort to provide would-be hustlers and dope dealers with an attractive alternative to the streets.

But even if one takes Cose at his word and moves from abject denial to a serious consideration of how the fates of black overachievers and potential dope dealers are linked, what would be the result? Does he, for example, really believe that the unhappiness he documents among those blacks who labor—however unappreciated or unpromoted—for Fortune 500 companies has much to say to a black drop-out contemplating a life among the Crips and Bloods? Indeed, for all my quarrels with the Nation of Islam, I suspect Louis Farrakhan has a much sounder grip on what urban despair is and how one might address it.

Nonetheless, Cose's reminders of how intransigent racial stereotypes are and how long the shadow of injustice is deserve our collective attention, if only because they force us to conduct the racial debate in other than the shouts and whispers that, thus far, have dominated the discussion. In this regard, Ed Koch, yet another former New York City mayor Cose interviewed in the making of his book, is dead right: many whites fear that "if they talk honestly they'll be called a racist," while many blacks, he conjectured, were scared "they'd be called Uncle Toms." Indeed, one need go no further than affirmative action to hit upon a topic that has produced more than its share of shouts-and-whispers, but precious little thoughtful discussion. Here, Cose is an exception, not only because he readily admits that "like many black professionals, I find myself profoundly ambivalent on the question of affirmative action. I don't believe that it works very well, nor that it can be made to satisfy much of anyone," but also because he understands that "affirmative action has been made the scapegoat for a host of problems that many Americans simply don't wish to face up to; and that while a huge and largely phony public debate has raged over whether affirmative action is good or bad, the reality is much more nuanced and complex."

Once again, *denial* is Cose's watchword, as dozens of interviewees document his case that white America "just don't get it" in terms of just how pissed-off many middle-class blacks are. So we have the case of the trade association vice president who was given responsibility for little more than "minority affairs" or the partner in a law firm who contrasts the world of the sixties (where "you knew white people didn't like black folks") with the current situation in which race prejudice has been driven underground in ways both more subtle and more treacherous.

Cose, a contributing editor and essayist for *Newsweek*, brings considerable journalistic skills to the portraits-in-pain he assembles, but he is hardly a sociologist in the mold of an Andrew Hacker or even an oral historian like, say, Studs Terkel. For while those writers make some effort to be even-handed, Cose selects his "evidence" in ways that stack the cards and lead one to conclude that there is not a single reasonably happy member among the tens of thousands numbered in the black middle class. To be sure, those with a modicum of experience in corporate America, as well as those who keep their eye on the talk show circuit, know better, for if one thing is true about minorities, it is that they do not think, or act, in lockstep. Moreover, although Cose insists that "it seemed a blessing . . . that their good humor and high spirits had survived," the testimonies he recounts show little evidence of either. What we have, instead, are anecdotes filled with hurt and humiliation, smashed dreams and bitter memories. As a word, *rage* figured less prominently in their accounts than did, say, "shock," but, taken together, rage is what the interviews come to.

No doubt Cose figured that, given the focus on his study, a certain amount of overemphasis was necessary; but I think he may have collected as many liabilities as assets in the process. For the plain truth is that, with enough encouragement, each of us could come up with evidence that life can be unfair or at least not all we had imagined it would be, even with hard work and dedication on our part. None of us, black or white, lives in paradise, and I further suspect that most adults know this. Moreover, the black adults I know strike me as far more realistic, and certainly far more resilient, than the pampered, whining types who often figure in Cose's narratives.

Do my last sentences put me squarely in the camp of the deniers? I think not, partly because I agree with Cose about the largely covert turn that racism has taken, and partly because I know its subtle manifestations can, and do, take their toll on the human spirit. Where we differ is in our sense of balancing how much has been accomplished against how much yet needs to be done, and where our priorities with regard to the latter ought to be. True enough, the Civil Rights Movement has not ushered in the milennium. Perhaps the dream Martin Luther King, Jr. dared to dream, and that millions dreamed along with him, will forever escape a country so deeply, tragically, rooted in the soil of racism. But Cose will have to forgive me for feeling that efforts to close the gap between our ideals as a nation and our less than noble conduct are still worth the making; and that the very stories he serves up as cautionary tales strike me as more akin to inspirations. For if opportunity and hard work have led to the spectacular careers he chronicles, surely the possibility of further progress in the difficult business of talking to each other exists.

Here, our viewpoints may not be so far apart after all, for Cose ends his book by arguing that the civil rights debate has been "distorted by strategies designed to engender guilt" and that a more intelligent debate might result if the slate were somehow to be magically wiped clean. History suggests that this is probably a tall order, but one worth trying if only because Cose is surely right when he insists that racism is less a construct than a quotidian condition, and that "the often hurtful and seemingly trivial encounters of daily existence are in the end what most of life is." One would not easily encounter such a well-turned, and deeply human, phrase in a scholarly tome on racism, and even though I continue to feel that black life, like all life, includes much more than one hurtful encounter piled atop another, I am grateful that the listening and the dialogue Cose recommends has at long last begun.

Home Boys Between Hard Covers

Parallel Time: Growing Up in Black and White. By Brent Staples. Pantheon Books. $23.00.

Makes Me Wanna Holler: A Black Man in America. By Nathan McCall. Random House. $23.00.

Colored People: A Memoir. By Henry Louis Gates, Jr. Knopf. $22.00.

> In the same way that Shelley saw all poems as fragments of one vast ur-poem, we see the black memoirist's tale as part of a larger, subsuming saga—an entry in the vast, multivolume project of Narrating the Negro.
>
> —Henry Louis Gates, Jr.

Memoirs can be as slippery as they are wide ranging, not only because the voices that tug our sleeve for attention often straddle the thin line separating fiction from autobiography, but also because memoirs cover such a large territory—everything from backward glances by the rich and culturally famous to accounts of "how it was" by out-of-work politicians. The books under discussion suggest yet another grouping: chronicles of suffering and despair penned by those who miraculously escaped their probable fates. Black memoirists thus give a palpable shape to those who, despite our national fixation on race, tend to remain largely invisible and who remain a "problem" rather than a people with problems. In short, their chronicles not only add to what Gates rightly calls the "vast, multivolume project entitled Narrating the Negro"—a tradition that includes such defining works as Frederick Douglass's *Narrative* and Richard Wright's *Black Boy*—but they also provide, for their predominantly white audience, a double-edged testimony that speaks to an individual writer's liberation from powerlessness and silence, as well as for the unprivileged who remain entrapped.

Those who equate memoir with writers of a certain age will gaze at the jacket photos of Nathan McCall, Brent Staples, and Henry Louis Gates, Jr. with bemused wonderment for what strikes one immediately is how *young* each of them is. Have they lived enough, experienced enough, indeed, *accomplished* enough to warrant publication, much less the lavish public attention that followed each of their books? The conventional answer, of course, is "No!" but I would submit that the recent crop of young black memoirists constitutes a special—albeit, complicated—case, partly because they are simultaneously survivors of, and witnesses to, all that is dehumanizing about contemporary black life in America, and partly because their words can be an entry point into experiences most white Americans absorb, if at all, through the distorting filters of the news media and popular entertainment.

In short, black memoirists hold forth the promise of a deeper truth, one with a point of view about the past and an understanding of how its particulars shaped the individual writer's consciousness. Not surprisingly, some writers succeed in this complicated venture more than others, for the art required of a real memoir, as opposed to the merely dashed-off or as-told-to varieties, is in the details—those selected as well as those withheld; and how the former are first nuanced and then shaped into a coherent whole. *Any* would-be memoirist faces these considerable obstacles; but if the writer happens to be black, there are additional challenges. How, for example, does one cobble the aesthetic distancing memoir demands with what McCall's title suggests is an equally legitimate need to "holler"; and how can one construct a balance between what W. E. B. DuBois long ago recognized as the essential twoness that struggles inside every black American soul?

Fortunately, these very conditions, vexing though they are, have been a source of richness and often the impetus for black writing as engaged as it is eloquent. Indeed, one could make similar claims about the grinding conditions of American life, arguing that black history is filled with examples of dignity rather than despair, of ordinary people turned into heroes by the long, uninterrupted struggle for freedom. My worry—*our* worry—is that Americans, both black and white, have forgotten how desperately bad social conditions were a mere forty years ago, and that the integration promised, and largely delivered, by the *Brown vs. the Board of Education* decision has given way to versions of black-promoted segregation, some militantly separatist, some merely voluntary, and the shrill cadences of a fashionable, often wildly inappropriate, rage. If black memoirs are to be measured by how much hatred they can pack into their paragraphs and how much white liberal guilt such screeds can generate, the result will not just spell trouble for talented black writers, but more important, continuing grief for us all.

I begin with these caveats because one cannot read *Parallel Time*, Brent Staples's account of his long-delayed grieving at his brother's death (like far, far too many young black men, he was murdered in a drug deal gone sour) without feeling that the parallels insisted upon are often extended efforts to replace responsibility with rage and free will with what James Baldwin once called the "doom" of color. The result is a book that proceeds by a series of story lines which, however close, do not quite touch: his brother's tragic destiny and the author's unrepresentative fate; the narrowing character of small-town Chester, PA, and the wider cultural orbits to be found at the University of Chicago; and perhaps most of all, what it means to grow up black as opposed to white.

No doubt white liberals will find Staples's account of how he made his way to a position on the *New York Times* affecting (read: guilt-producing), for how else could they possibly read the attention-grabbing paragraph that sets *Parallel Time* into motion:

> My brother's body lies dead and naked on a stainless steel slab. At his head stands a tall arched spigot that, with tap handles mimicking wings, easily suggests a swan in mourning. His head is squarish and overlarge. (Thus, when he was a toddler, made him seem top-heavy and unsteady on his feet.) His widow's peak is common among the men in my family, though this one is more dramatic than most. An inverted pyramid, it begins high above the temples and falls steeply to an apex in the boxy forehead, over the heart-shaped face. A triangle into a box over a heart. His eyes (closed here) were big and dark and glittery; they drew you into his sadness when he cried. The lips were ajar as always, but the picture is taken from such an angle that it misses a crucial detail: the left front tooth tucked partly beyond the right one. I need this detail to see my brother full. I paint it in from memory.

Staples's account may mean to be arresting, even melodramatic, but it is not ghoulish; for the bullet-ridden body on the slab—his little brother, Blake—is a trope for black manhood cut down in its prime, the emblematic victim of a world he did not make and could not overcome. The coroner's photograph is dated 13 February 1984, a time when Brent Staples was half a country away, pursuing a doctorate in psychology at the University of Chicago. He did not attend the funeral, and even more significantly, was not able to turn what he had learned about clinical psychology to his own case. Only later, when a dismal job market forced him to try his hand at free-lance writing and then to a career in journalism, did he circle back, not only telling the story of their parallel lives, but also finally coming to terms with his grief.

To his credit, Staples is an eagle-eyed writer with an elephant's thick skin; but such assets have come at a considerable human cost. As the oldest of nine children, he watched his family's downward spiral—everything from evictions that forced them to move from one dwelling to the next (once a landlord unceremoniously hauled their furnishings out to the street) to outbursts of domestic violence. His father, a truck driver, was usually drunk; a wild sister ran away; a cousin was shot; and his mother suffering through it all, including a horrifying moment Staples describes this way:

> One night my mother screamed. . . . My father had drawn a knife and cut her. The wound took several stitches to close. Later, after it had healed, I helped her remove the stitches. The cut was awkwardly placed, toward the back side of her upper left arm. I held a mirror to the wound so that she could see to cut the suture knots. The stitches were black. A collar of dried pus clung to their necks as she pulled them out.

Staples describes how the wound looked and the configuration that pus along the sutures made with a matter-of-fact, clinical precision, but curiously enough, not how it felt when his mother was so assaulted. Moreover, such distanced, dry reportage becomes the book's pattern. The result is that everything, pleasant and unpleasant, is given the same unemotional treatment. One possibility, of course, is that the rigorous understatement is purposeful, a latter-day version of Hemingway's tight-lipped style, but I suspect that it generates from quite other sources—namely, Staples's inability to confront his childhood with *emotional* honesty.

For the truth about Staples's youthful world is that it was a dangerous place, and this in an age before gangs, drive-by shootings, or AIDS. The streets, the local bars, the largely segregated neighborhoods (blacks on one side of town, Ukranians and Poles on the other), even the schools made parallel lives de facto, if not always explicit. And if Staples makes sure that we write him down as a politicized hellraiser during his days at Widener College, it is also clear that he was always a reader, a serious student, and most of all, somebody who wanted *out*.

When he finally left, Staples took a good deal of emotional baggage—what, in Chester, would be called an "attitude" —with him. How could that not be, given the smoldering resentments he felt about his abusive father and excuse-making mother, his siblings, his white [racist] classmates, and himself? But that said, it is the "himself" that Staples studiously avoids confronting, opting instead to pad his memoir with new installments and fresh villains: college trustees who neither "get it" nor *trust* him; newspaper editors who anger him at interviews or on the job; and finally, even Saul Bellow himself, a man Staples hunts down because he wants to pluck the heart out of his creative mystery, but also because he finds his black characters so disturbing.

The section on Bellow has occassioned a good deal of commentary, and rightly so—for there is something unseemly, even dangerous, in *Parallel Time*'s glib equation of character and author, to say nothing of the compulsive rage that resulted. Staples clearly admires Bellow's fiction, and like many another University of Chicago graduate student, he took a peculiar delight in the insider gossip about how, say, sociologist Edward Shils had been first artistically kidnapped and then smuggled into the pages of *Humboldt's Gift* as Professor Richard Durnwald. However, these delights soon paled when the novel turns abruptly from mild farce to incipient racism—"when a black man steps out of the shadows and, with no motive, slits a white woman's throat," and when Bellow betrays a side Staples had not realized heretofore:

> Black people in the book were sinister characters. Rinaldo refers to them as "crazy buffaloes" and "pork chops." Crazy buffaloes populate the slums that surround Hyde Park. A pork chop chases Charlie down the middle of his street, presumably at night. These passages made me angry. It was the same anger I felt when white people cowered past me on the street.

Add the controversial scene from *Mr. Sammler's Planet* in which a princely black pickpocket exposes himself and Staples's suspicions are more than confirmed: "Bellow wanted the dick remembered. He returned to it again and again as a symbol of spiritual decay, of the 'sexual niggerhood' that 'millions of civilized people' had deluded themselves in wanting." His disappointment ("I expected more of a man who could see to the soul") soon turns to outrage, and then to a loopy plan to confront Bellow near his apartment building—in effect, degrading the degarder, kidnapping the kidnapper:

> Now and then I bounded up the tower stairs [of his apartment] to make sure Bellow's name was still on the bell: A security gate cuts you off from the base of the tower itself, which was too bad, because there were shadows to linger in. His neighbors suffered mightily from my visits, especially when they encountered me descending the stairs in the dark.
>
> What would I do when I caught him? Perhaps I'd lift him bodily and pin him against a wall. Perhaps I'd corner him on the stairs and take up questions about "pork chops" and "crazy buffaloes" and barbarous black pickpockets. I wanted to trophy his fear.

Fortunately, Staples's "stalking" (his term, by the way) comes to no avail, but for a man who now seeks attention as a *writer*, the episode remains unsettling—not because Bellow was in physical danger or Staples's anger was justified (it wasn't), but, rather, because he recounts the incident with neither recognition nor shame. One could, of course, suggest that he might have plumbed Bellow's depths more deeply had he simply checked out other Bellow novels from the library and read them more carefully than he obviously had *Mr. Sammler's Planet* and *Humboldt's Gift*; but that would be to take Staples's talent seriously, and in ways that most of the reviewers of *Parallel Lives* did not.

Something of the same giddy excitement about the underbelly of black life coupled with a craven refusal to apply the usual standards of human decency when judging a black memoirist's "I" also surrounds Nathan McCall's *It Makes Me Wanna Holler*. Indeed, given the way black rage is currently subdivided, McCall's book beats *Parallel Time* hands down, for it not only sports a "hero" who did hard time, rather than graduate study, before becoming a professional journalist, but also provides an insider's account of black street life that makes Staples's Chester look like Eden. It is the difference between that which makes you want to cry (although Staples could not do that, if at all, until the last pages) and that which makes you "wanna holler," the irritants that cause Staples to fantasize about pushing Bellow up against the wall and the rage that gives an ugly animus to McCall's opening paragraphs:

> The fellas and I were hanging out on our corner one afternoon when the strangest thing happened. A white boy, who appeared to be about eighteen or nineteen years old, came pedaling a bicycle casually through the neighborhood. I don't know if he was lost or just confused, but he was definitely in the wrong place to be doing the tourist bit. Somebody spotted him and pointed him out to the rest of us. "Look! What's that motherfucka doin' ridin' through here?! Is he *crraaaazy*?!"
>
> It was automatic. We all took off after him. We caught him on Cavalier Boulevard and knocked him off the bike. He fell to the ground and it was all over. We were on him like white on rice. Ignoring the passing cars, we stomped him and kicked him. My stick partners kicked him in the head and face and watched the blood gush from his mouth. I kicked him in the stomach and nuts, where I knew it would hurt. Every time I drove my foot into his balls, I felt better; with each blow delivered, I gritted my teeth as I remembered some recent racial sight:
>
> THIS is for all the times you followed me round in stores. . . . And THIS is for the times you treated me like a nigger. . . . And *THIS is for G.P.—General Principle—just 'cause you white.*

The gut-wrenching power the scene packs is repeated again and again as McCall describes what it was like, *really* like, to be a young black man in America: on one hand, the rigorous, internal codes governing everything from shooting hoops to "setting up a train" (read: gang bang), the complicated network of language and gestures that signified "respect," and, of course, the dabbling in drugs and crime that turned many of his comrades into grim statistics; and on the other, the insidious ways that racist America spawned a rage and loathing only matched by its capacity to generate oceans of self-hatred.

Because what I've just described makes McCall's book sound like a guided tour through the darker alleys of black pathology, let me hasten to add that its author also intends his story to be a chronicle of transformation and triumph, for the street punk who misspent his youth ultimately becomes, like Brent Staples, a journalist for a major newspaper—in McCall's case, the *Washington Post.* Given the sheer arc of such a life, there is no end of ways that its unfolding might have become compromised, either by an insistence that he recognized more than the brutal facts of his youth suggest, or by appeals to the court of public opinion on the grounds of victimization. Generally speaking, *It Makes Me Holler* avoids most of the first traps; McCall, in short, has little interest in efforts to make his unreconstructed self more sensitive, more humane, if you will, than he really was—and the young McCall was, by any measure, *baad.* At 14, gang fights and gang bangs, muggings and petty theft were the marching orders of his tribe; and while McCall did not end up on a mortician's slab, he allows us to see, and moreover, to *feel* how such meaningless deaths commonly happen:

> Moving close enough for me to smell his breath, Plaz poked a finger in my chest. . . . "I'll kick your ass. . . !"
>
> In one swift motion, I drew the gun, aimed it point-blank at his chest, and fired. *Bam!* . . . In that moment, I felt like God. I felt so good and powerful that I wanted to do it again. I felt like I could pull that trigger, and keep on pulling it until I emptied the gun. Years later, I read an article in a psychology magazine that likened the feeling of shooting a gun to ejaculation. That's what it was like for me. Shooting off.

Small wonder that this McCall, the creature of impulse and confusion, has been trotted out as a latter-day Bigger Thomas, or that his remarkable transmogrification into an articulate, purposeful person has been likened to that of Malcolm X. For no black memoirist apparently operates on his own, outside—much less beyond—the defining tradition of slave narratives and such formative texts as Richard Wright's *Black Boy* and *Native Son,* Baldwin's essays, Claude Brown's *Manchild in the Promised Land,* and *The Autobiography of Malcolm X.* Indeed, McCall himself recognizes this interlocking kinship in a scene—arguably the most defining one in the book—that forces him to recognize his fate as reflected through the prism of Bigger Thomas's desperate eyes:

> I identified strongly with Bigger and the book's narrative. He was twenty, the same age as me. He felt the things I felt, and, like me, he wound up in prison. The book's portrait of Bigger captured all those conflicting feelings—restless anger, hopelessness, a tough facade among blacks and a deep-seated fear of whites—that I'd sensed in myself but was unable to express. Often, during my teenaged years, I'd felt like Bigger—headed down a road toward a destruction I couldn't ward off,

> beaten by forces so large and amorphous that I had no idea how to fight back. I was surprised that somebody had written a book that so closely reflected my experiences and feelings.

For white readers—and talk about black literary traditions aside, it's clear that McCall's book has been packaged for them—this extraordinary passage has a salutary effect, for if a former brute can speak so knowingly, so eloquently, perhaps there is hope, after all. But while I freely admit that I would much prefer chatting with *this* McCall, the one of books and words, rather than the scary hooligan who took enormous pleasure in "fucking up white boys"—that is, beating them senseless—I also suspect that, given the evidence of the book's final chapters, we would probably not chat very long before both of us would become exasperated—in McCall's case, because my praise would sound patronizing and my criticism, racist; and in mine, because I could not look at him without recalling Baldwin's memories (in *The Fire Next Time*) of himself as a wildly successful boy preacher: "That was the most frightening time of my life, and quite the most dishonest, and the resulting hysteria lent great passion to my sermons—for a while, I relished the attention and the relative immunity from punishment that my new status gave me."

In a review written for the pages of the *New Yorker* magazine, Henry Louis Gates, Jr., arguably the country's most distinguished black literary critic, interrupts his bright talk about McCall's book and the way it turns a Bigger Thomas into a Richard Wright, to include a paragraph that says as much, indeed, perhaps more, about Gates than his ostensible subject:

> I read "Makes Me Wanna Holler" with a sense of both recognition and consternation. McCall and I are only a few years apart in age, so I share his cultural references; my old man, like his, was an unskilled worker who held two jobs. The warm-bath intimacy of the all-black world that McCall grew up in is familiar to me. But as for how a Bigger Thomas emerged from all this, McCall ultimately doesn't have a clue, and neither do I.

Indeed, what distinguishes Gate's memoir from those of Staples and McCall is a sense of nostalgia for, rather than a yearning to escape from, the cultural conditions of his childhood. Or put another way, Gates is comfortable with his blackness in ways that most black memoirists are not. One indicator is his title, meant to evoke the sepia tones of an earlier, innocent age at the same time it coyly tweaks the noses of those who now insist that "colored people" is déclassé while *persons of color* is du rigeur; another is his admission, after a lifetime as a professional "race man," that he no longer tries "to tell other Negroes how to be black." Yet another difference, perhaps the most telling of them all, is the way he invites his readers into a consideration of what life among the "colored people" of Piedmont, West Virginia, was like during the years before the civil rights movement changed life there, and elsewhere, forever. Rather than images of a dead drug dealer or pummelled white boy, Gates launches his highly selective narrative with a letter to his young daughters, at once an effort to reanimate Piedmont before its paper mill closes down and the town itself dies, and an attempt to answer their questions about the civil rights movement itself. On a drive back to Piedmont, Gates had pointed to a motel on Route 2 and said

> that at one time I could not have stayed there. Your mother [who is white] could have stayed there, but your mother couldn't have stayed with me. And you kids looked at us like we were telling you the biggest lie you had ever heard. So I thought about writing to you.

Granted, the ploy is as patently artificial as Gates's memories are highly selective (he does not, for example, tell us more about how his exogamous relationship played out with her family, much less with his; nor will this memoir include insider gossip about his life as a celebrated academic; these installments will, presumably, come later), but it does clearly establish the time and place Gates means to explore.

The Piedmont of Gates's memory was a small town (22,000 souls, 351 of them colored) nestled in the Allegheny Mountains, a place of natural beauty and measures of economic prosperity, where whites and blacks got along (largely because both knew their place, and neither challenged what had long been accepted), and perhaps most of all, where everybody knew, and harbored strong opinions about, everybody else:

> You couldn't get away with anything in Piedmont. Most people just did it as discretely as they could, knowing not only that everybody colored knew but also that their name would be in the streets every day, permanently and forever, whenever the conversation lagged, new business being over, and old business was called up to pass the time.

All this, of course, is by way of stating the obvious—namely, that Piedmont was a *very small* small town, enough to make anyone with bigger eyes feel suffocated, but in Gates's case, also the stuff of which community, and character, were made. For whatever else the 1950's represented, its essential innocence retains an enormous power, one Gates evokes in cultural memories so honest and humanly palpable that only an ideologue of the first water would dismiss them as politically incorrect:

> "Colored, colored, on Channel Two," you'd hear someone shout. Somebody else would run to the phone, while yet another hit the front porch, telling all the neighbors where to see it. And *everybody* loved *Amos and Andy*—I don't care what people say today. For the colored people, the day they took *Amos and Andy* off the air was one of the saddest days in Piedmont, about as sad as the day of the last mill pic-a-nic.
>
> What was special to us about *Amos and Andy* was that their world was all colored, just like ours. Of course, they had their colored judges and lawyers and doctors and nurses, which we could only dream about having, or becoming—and we did dream about those things. . . . As far as we were concerned, the foibles of Kingfish or Calhoun the lawyer were the foibles of individuals who happened to be funny. Nobody was likely to confuse them with the colored people we knew, no more than we'd confuse ourselves with the entertainers and athletes we saw on TV or in *Ebony* or *Jet*, the magazines we devoured to keep up with what was happening with the race. And people took special relish in Kingfish's malapropisms. "I deny the allegation, Your honor, and I resents the alligator."

As I said, a culturally innocent time, especially when compared with the coarser moments most black memoirists recount, but Saul Bellow—to invoke his name again—is not the only American writer to have a character (in this case, Moses Herzog) ask why only *brutal* reality gets a hearing, as if no other adjectives are authentic; Henry Louis Gates, Jr. is clearly another.

And yet, for all the fishing and hunting trips, warmly recounted, all the mature acceptance of a world with its share of parochialism and warts, there are also jarring notes—foreshadowings, if you will—of the racial animosity that had always existed among Piedmont's colored folk, and that finally seeped into their living rooms through the same television set that had brought them episodes of *Amos and Andy*. Perhaps the young Gates's biggest shock came when he realized that not only did his mother refuse to fear white people, but also that she actively *hated* them:

> There were rare occasions when I would look into her face and see a stranger. In 1959, when I was nine, Mike Wallace and CBS aired a documentary about Black Muslims. It was called "The Hate That Hate Produced," and these were just about the scariest black people I'd ever seen. Black people who talked right into the faces of white people, telling them off without even blinking. While I sat cowering in our living room, I happened to glance over at my mother. A certain radiance was slowly transforming her soft brown face, as she listened to Malcolm X naming the white man the Devil. "Amen," she said, quietly at first. "All right now," she continued, much more heatedly. All this time, and I hadn't known just how deeply my mother despised white people. It was like watching the Wicked Witch of the West emerge out of the transforming figure of Dorothy. The revelation was both terrifying and thrilling.

To be sure, this Gates, the one simultaneously shocked out of and initiated into the black American's complex fate, soon gives way to a sadder, wiser version who realizes that, although "all things considered, white and colored Piedmont got along pretty well in those years, the fifties and early sixties," the gains from this relationship were clearly stacked on one side and the losses on the other. It was, in short, a racial formula that depended on a whole litany of as-long-as's—"as long as colored people didn't try to sit down in the Cut-Rate . . . or buy property, or move into the white neighborhoods, or dance with, date, or dilate upon white people."

Integration would, of course, disrupt the equilibrium, and change the separate-but-never equal worlds of Piedmont's white folks and colored people forever. Later, the riots in Watts offered up even greater shocks, ones which altered the social dynamic every bit as much as the town's decaying paper mill would later. As usual, the catastrophic events on the other side of the country entered Piedmont's collective consciousness via television, but this time they caught Gates while he was at Peterkin, an integrated Episcopal summer church camp filled with smart, questioning, generous-spirited teenagers like himself. For two blissful weeks, they had made real progress toward seeing each other as individuals, without the impediments of the color line, which W. E. B. DuBois had insisted would be the 20th century's deepest, most recalcitrant problem. Such harmony is both fragile and beautiful—and, alas, always threatened by the crush of events more incendiary than bonfires and sing-alongs:

> What the news of the riots did for us was to remind everybody in one fell swoop that there was a racial context outside Peterkin that affected relations between white and black Americans; we had suddenly to remember that our roles were scripted by that larger context. We had for a blissful week been functioning as best we could, that is—when all of a sudden the context had come crashing down upon us once again. I hated that newspaper. But we overcame it: with difficulty, with perseverance, we pushed away the racial context and could interact not as allegories but as people. It felt like something of an achievement.

Colored People may restrict its scope to a time and place that springs to life only on the printed page, but that would be to sell Gates's memoir short—for one also has the feeling that its vivid characters continue to speak in paragraphs that have their thumbprint on every word:

> I want to be able to take special pride in a Jessye Norman aria, a Muhammad Ali shuffle, a Michael Jordan slam dunk, a Spike Lee movie, a Thurgood Marshall opinion, a Toni Morrison novel, James Brown's Camel Walk. Above all, I enjoy the unselfconscious moments of a shared cultural intimacy, whatever form they take, when no one else is watching. Like Joe Louis's fights, which my father still talks about as part of the fixed repertoire of stories that texture our lives. You've seen his eyes shining as he describes how Louis hit Max Schmeling so many times and so hard, and how some reporter asked him, after the fight: "Joe, what would you have done if that last punch hadn't knocked Schmeling out?" And how ole Joe responded, without missing a beat: "I'd run around behind him to see what was holdin' him up!"
>
> Even so, I rebel at the notion that I can't be part of other groups, that I can't construct identities through elective affinity, that race must be the most important thing about me. Is that what I want on my gravestone: Here lies an African American? So I'm divided. I want to be black, to know black, to luxuriate in whatever I might be calling blackness at any particular time—but to do so in order to come out the other side, to experience a humanity that is neither colorless nor reducible to color. Bach *and* James Brown, Sushi *and* fried catfish. Part of me admires those people who can say with a straight face that they have transcended any attachment to a particular community or group . . . but I always want to run around behind them to see what holds them up.

If the memoirs by Staples and McCall contribute their share to the continuing Narrative of the Negro, so, too, I would argue, does Gates—but with this essential difference: *Colored People* is less a story of survival and escape than one in which memory can wear the robes of love and the achievement he once felt at a summer camp can be reduplicated over and over again. There should be room for such testimonies, if for no other reason than the simple, indisputable fact that all of us, black and white alike, need them.

What's Love, and Candor, Got To Do With It?

Race Matters. By Cornell West. Beacon Press. $15.00.

Race Matters may be a slim volume, but it has propelled its author to wide public attention, not only because the eight essays collected between its hard covers deal with such controversial issues as black-Jewish relations, black rage, and the crisis in black leadership, or even because its publication date coincided with the first anniversary of the profound social unrest that exploded in south central Los Angeles, but also because the book makes it clear that West is an intellectual in the best sense of the term. His passionate commitment to a wide range of ideas and perhaps more important, to the humanistic implications of those ideas help to sharpen a debate at the very center of our culture, and demand that his clear, eloquent prose be taken seriously.

For West, the rhetoric of liberals and conservatives alike is no longer equal to the task of social analysis, much less to the challenges that white racism and versions of black separatism continue to pose. Both those who align themselves with the liberal notion that "more government programs can solve racial problems" and those conservatives who argue that what is needed "is a change in the moral behavior of poor black urban dwellers" miss what West regards as the essential point—namely, that blacks are not, in the words of Dorothy I. Height, president of the National Council of Negro Women, a "problem people," but rather "fellow American citizens with problems."

Hence, his insistence that what the times require is nothing less than a "new framework," one that begins with a frank acknowledgement of the basic humanness and Americanness of each of us, and that then goes on to acknowledge that "as a people—*E Pluribus Unum*—we are on a slippery slope toward economic strife, social turmoil, and cultural chaos." Unless the trajectory is reversed—by replacing hatred with love and political cant with unflinching candor—all of us, blacks and whites alike, are doomed to a collective fate: "*If we go down, we go down together*." That single, riveting sentence speaks volumes about West's capacity for moral argument and prophetic vision. It also suggests something of why *Race Matters* will "matter" to those who often find themselves paralyzed by the racial nightmare from which most Americans can never fully awaken. As West points out, "The Los Angeles upheaval [he insists it was neither a race riot nor a class rebellion] forced us to see not only that we are not connected in ways we would like to be but also, in a more profound sense, that this failure to connect binds us even more tightly together."

This much said, however, let me hasten to add that West is no more immune from bouts of despair than the rest of us. Indeed, his "Preface" begins with the way that certain observations by Plato and W. E. B. DuBois continue to haunt him:

> In a mysterious way, this classic twosome posed the most fundamental challenges to my basic aim in life: to speak the truth to power with love so that the quality of everyday life for ordinary people is enhanced and white supremacy is stripped of its authority and legitimacy. Plato's profound—yet unpersuasive—critique of Athenian democracy as inevitably corrupted by the ignorance and passions of the masses posed one challenge, and DuBois's deep analysis of the intransience of white supremacy in the American democratic experiment posed another.

West means to stake out a higher moral ground, one that holds fast to the best that America can be at the same time that it refuses to blink in the face of the worst that American life all too often is. West, after all, has been the beneficiary and victim of both sides of the vexing coin—at once a distinguished professor at Princeton University (where he teaches in the religion department and chairs its Afro-American Studies Program) and a black man subject to daily, humiliating reminders that skin color, rather than intellect, is what counts.

Indeed, the latter experiences are so painful that he recounts them in some detail, beginning with the ten taxicabs that refused to pick him up on a Manhattan corner and then moving backward to the time he was stopped on false charges of trafficking cocaine (when West told the officer he was a professor of religion, the policeman replied, "Yeh, and I'm the Flying Nun.

Let's go, nigger!"). Nor is pastoral Princeton, New Jersey an exception. Drive its streets too slowly and you will discover—that is, if you happen to be black—that being pulled over, hassled, and sometimes searched is standard procedure. During his first ten days as a new member of Princeton's faculty, West made precisely that discovery three times. The "lessons," shall we say, were not lost on him, although he quickly adds that these incidents, enraging as they might be, "are dwarfed by those like Rodney King's beating or the abuse of black targets of the FBI's COINTELPRO efforts in the 1960s and 1970s."

Nonetheless, West's memories hurt and scar his soul. So it is hardly surprising that he is obsessed by "what *race* matters have meant to the American past and of how much race *matters* in the American present." In this case, the play on words is more than academic cleverness; rather it is, for West, "an urgent question of power and morality" and for others, "an everyday matter of life and death." Thus, nihilism—at least as the term is applied to black communities—needs to be defined less as a philosophic doctrine arguing that there are no rational grounds for legitimate standards or authority than as the "*lived experience of coping with a life of horrifying meaninglessness, hopelessness, and (most important) lovelessness.*" Granted, the latter brand of nihilism is hardly new—West points out that the first African encounter with the New World was a distinctive form of the Absurd—but the genius of black foremothers and forefathers

> . . . was to create powerful buffers to ward off the nihilistic threat, to equip black folk with cultural armor to beat back the demons of hopelessness, meaninglessness, and lovelessness. . . . In other words, traditions for blacks surviving and thriving under usually adverse New World conditions were major barriers against the nihilistic threat. These traditions consist primarily of black religious and civic institutions that sustained familial and communal networks of support. If cultures are, in part, what human beings create (out of antecedent fragments of other cultures) in order to convince themselves not to commit suicide, then black foremothers and forefathers are to be applauded.

But at a moment when young black people lead the nation in suicides, West is hardly alone in asking "What has gone wrong?" Is it, as some would claim, the bitter irony of integration, or as others insist, the cumulative effects of a genocidal conspiracy? Both views certainly "play" on the mean streets and among those who have hitched their political wagons to separatism. And of course there are those who would point to the rising expectations set into motion during the giddy, optimistic days of the 1960s and claim that a certain amount of "downsizing" is inevitable. By contrast, West believes that there are two significant reasons why the threats of nihilism are more powerful now than ever before: one is the "saturation of market forces and market moralities in black life" while the other is nothing more nor less than "a present crisis in black leadership."

With regard to the first, West ticks off the images of comfort, convenience, machismo, femininity, violence, and sexual stimulation that bombard black consumers and serve to fatten corporate profits. Thus, market institutions

> have greatly contributed to undermining traditional morality. . . . [Moreover], the reduction of individuals to objects of pleasure is especially evident in the culture industries—television, radio, video, music—in which gestures of sexual foreplay and orgiastic pleasure flood the marketplace. . . .

As West would have it, black Americans are especially susceptible to these seductive images, with the result that a market-inspired life effectively edges out those "non-market values—love, care, service to others"—that formerly sustained black communities. Much of this sounds as if West were making common cause with the Allan Bloom who took mindless pleasures to task in *The Closing of the American Mind*, but West has quite another agenda up his sleeve, for he means to eradicate black nihilism through a strategy of love and caring he calls a "*politics of conversion*." Here, it seems to me, West is on firmer ground, in the sense that religious values, rather than economic systems, are his forte. Nonetheless, it is harder to see how this "politics of conversion" would actually work than it is to notice how he has cobbled aspects of liberal and neoconservative thought into his analysis:

> Like liberal structuralists, the advocates of a politics of conversion never lose sight of the structural conditions that shape the sufferings and lives of people. Yet, unlike liberal structuralism, the politics of conversion meets the nihilistic threat head-on. Like conservative behaviorism, the politics of conversion openly confronts the self-destructive and inhumane actions of black people. Unlike conservative behaviorists, the politics of conversion situates these actions within inhumane circumstances (but does not thereby exonerate them).

West's idealism is more persuasive when its target is the failure of nerve all too often exhibited by black leaders. Writing about the Clarence Thomas/Anita Hill hearings, what strikes him as remarkable is the way that "Bush's choice of Thomas caught most black leaders off guard":

> Few had the courage to say publicly that this was an act of cynical tokenism concealed by outright lies about Thomas being the most qualified candidate regardless of race. . . . The very fact that no black leader could utter publicly that a black appointee for the Supreme Court was *unqualified* shows how captive they are to white racist stereotypes about black intellectual talent.

If generous doses of *love* are what the black underclass most desperately needs, it is also clear that *candor* is largely missing in the political rhetoric, and often in the discourse of black intellectuals. With the notable exception of Henry Louis Gates, Jr., few have spoken out against the black anti-Semitism peddled by hate merchants such as Leonard Jeffries or Louis Farrakhan. West is clearly troubled by the nasty turn that black-Jewish relations has taken but feels it is time to move beyond both vulgar name-calling and self-righteous finger-pointing. For the deeper truth, West insists, is that "black anti-Semitism and Jewish antiblack racism are real, and both are as profoundly American as cherry pie. There was no *golden age* in which blacks and Jews were free of tension and friction." But there was, West also insists, "a better age when the common histories of oppression and degradation of both groups served as a springboard for genuine empathy and principled alliances." To ask why, since the late 60s, black-Jewish relations have steadily deteriorated is rather akin to his earlier query about why black communities have fallen into nihilism.

West begins, quite properly, with an admission that "few blacks recognize and acknowledge one fundamental fact of Jewish history: a profound hatred of Jews sits at the center of medieval and modern European communities." Indeed, long before the word "ghetto" was associated with poor urban blacks, walled gates were an ugly fact of life for most European Jews. That much admitted, however, West goes on to insist that the history of Jews in America "flies in the face of this tragic past," and, moreover, that "the astonishingly rapid entree of most Jews into the middle and upper middle classes" between 1910 and 1967 now serves to divide those who favor affirmative action programs from those who oppose them. The State of Israel has only exacerbated the problem because "without a sympathetic understanding of the deep historic sources of Jewish fears and anxieties about group survival, blacks will not grasp the visceral attachment of most Jews to Israel." By the same token, "without a candid acknowledgement of blacks' status as permanent underdogs in American society, Jews will not comprehend what the symbolic predicament and literal plight of Palestinians in Israel means to blacks."

What both groups need to recognize, then, is the "moral content of Jewish and black identities and of their political consequences," for if it is true that blacks have been in the forefront of the struggle against American racism, it is also true that "if these efforts fall prey to anti-Semitism, then the principled attempt to combat racism forfeits much of its moral credibility—and we all lose." Thus,

> The vicious murder of Yankel Rosenbaum in Crown Heights in the summer of 1991 bore chilling testimony to a growing black anti-Semitism in this country. Although this particular form of xenophobia from below does not have the same institutional power of those racisms that afflict their victims from above, it certainly deserves the same moral condemnation. Furthermore, the very *ethical* character of the black freedom struggle largely depends on the open condemnation by its spokespersons of any racist attitude or action.

That West does not quibble in his condemnation of what happened in Crown Heights is good news, but it is even better news that black clergymen—from Reverend Gary Simpson of Concord Baptist Church in Brooklyn (with ten thousand members) and Reverend James Forbes of Riverside Church (with three thousand members) to a litany of others—have voiced similar opinions. Too often what the media serves up are "sound bites" from the angriest militants reports can corral. But as West reminds us, the best of black culture

> as manifested, for example, in jazz or the prophetic black church, refuses to put whites or Jews on a pedestal or in the gutter. Rather, black humanity is affirmed alongside that of others, even when those others have at times dehumanized blacks.

In an age when humanism itself often seems to be under attack, West's steady faith in the power of love and the necessity of candor is infectious. His reflections on why black anti-Semitism is unworthy and doomed to self-destruction is but one example of why *Race Matters* is such an extraordinary book. Indeed, one need only turn to his probing thoughts about the complicated psychological myths that surround black sexuality and the ways that black homophobia reinforce images of black machismo identity or to the various myths that have overtaken Malcolm X's life to feel the reassuring hand of his humanism. For what West represents is nothing more nor less than the black intellectual he has been looking for. Which is to say, if any notes in *Race Matters* ring false, they are probably those that rattle on about the vacuum in black intellectual leadership. West's essays make precisely the opposite case, not only putting him squarely in the tradition of black learning that produced the likes of W. E. B. DuBois and Oliver Cox, St. Claire Drake and Ralph Ellison, but also suggesting that one possibility of the "prophetic" is a future where those who share West's commitment to truth-telling and a better quality of life for all Americans might yet become a critical mass.

The Moose on the Family Dinner Table

Fatheralong: A Meditation on Fathers and Sons, Race and Society. By John Edgar Wideman. Pantheon. $21.00.

Race in America has been compared to a moose on the dining room table: nobody wants to call attention to the carcass despite the fact that antlers are sticking in the potatoes, hooves drip onto people's laps, and the smell keeps getting worse. Rather than acknowledge the obvious, people crane their necks around the rotting slab of flesh and ask those across the table to pass the salt.

John Edgar Wideman is a writer we've learned to trust when it comes to calling a moose a moose—that is, until *Fatheralong*. Ballyhooed as a meditation on "fathers and sons, race and society," Wideman watchers had good reasons to expect the same personal candor and sensitive trenchant social analysis he brought to *Brothers and Keepers*, his 1984 account of a brother jailed on a murder charge. How could the same family circumstances and Pittsburgh ghetto that produced *him*—a University of Pennsylvania graduate and Rhodes scholar: well spoken, ambitious, successful—also give rise to a brother who becomes a street punk and then one more sad statistic in the justice system? What propelled one brother toward restraint and standard English while the other gave way to jive talk and increasingly dangerous hussles: and what does this all say about the distancing, and the debts, a black writer owes to the black community?

I remember thinking that Wideman had sold himself a bit too short—and his brother a bit too long—in *Brothers and Keepers*, that even love is not enough to justify the unswerving defense he mounted on behalf of why so many young black men go bad. At the same time, I was moved by the painful honesty seared onto every page. So, when I learned that Wideman's own son was facing a murder charge, I wondered how the environmental arguments would play out when the situation seemed so radically altered. Unlike his brother, Wideman's son Jake was hardly the product of poverty and the inner city's meaner streets: he grew up in a successful academic's home, and in Laramie, Wyoming to boot.

Long before Murray and Herrnstein's *The Bell Curve* raised an already tense racial climate to new levels of accusation and hurt, Wideman must have ruminated about questions that can only crack the heart. Is racist America the sole reason why so many young black men murder, and are murdered—or are there other more complicated, more wrenching reasons? Given the sheer number of murderers in Wideman's family circle—including a nephew—one is tempted to think that genetic factors must be playing a role, as they do in families with a history of alcoholics. Granted, predisposition is only that—a predisposition—but it cannot be entirely ignored. Nor can the lessons, admittedly less scientific, from the histories of families seemingly fated to doom: the house of Atreus, the Kennedy clan, and now, the Widemans.

What I have been pointing to is nothing more nor less than the moose on the Wideman family dinner table, and the ways that *Fatheralong* skillfully avoids mentioning it until the book's last pages. It is one thing when *Philadelphia Fire* (1990) studiously avoids taking a position about MOVE and the conflagration that provided the novel's title (postmodernist narrative will do that) or when *Rueben* (1987) wraps coded messages about his son Jake in the folds of fiction and quite another when a book of non-fiction purports to talk about fathers, sons, and race and virtually leaves his son—now serving a life sentence—out.

Fatheralong is the mistaken way a very young John Edgar Wideman heard the gospel song "Farther Along," but it is also a talisman, a Rosetta stone, for the identity he still quests, and for the cold, distant father who remains an inexorable part of the equation:

> Till I was grown I heard "fatheralong" and thought Fatheralong was God's name in this hymn, the mysterious God who dwelled in Homewood A.M.E.Z. church, a God I'd meet up with some day and He'd understand and say Well done. Also, I thought of my father, Edgar Wideman, his doubleness, his two-personalities, a man who lived in our house, who in a way ruled it, yet also lived somewhere else, distant unknown.

Whatever the confusions, the song, Wideman argues, ultimately speaks the lessons "of resignation, learning to wait and trust and endure." In Wideman's case, father often seemed harsher, more remote than God; nor did the father-son relationship improve markedly during his adulthood. Things closest to the heart continued to be postponed, to remain unsaid. One mistake, Wideman now admits, was treating his father "as if a father always required a capital *F*." He then goes on to write this extraordinary passage:

> As long as I carried a deity, a natural force in my mind, I wouldn't see the man on the seat beside me. Why had it been impossible all these years to believe in this man's actual life, him with a suitcase in his hand, excited, anxious to get the hell away from the everyday tedium of growing old, alone and poor.

It took equal measures of courage and integrity to pen these lines; but these are precisely the benchmarks against which our best writers are judged. *Fatheralong* has more than its share of similar moments—when, for example, he visits with Wideman relatives at his grandfather's home in Greenwood, South Carolina, or when he meets his father at the train station near his Massachusetts home on the occasion of his son Danny's wedding. Family history, despite everything, exerts a palpable—and deeply poetic—force.

Families, in a word, *sustain*, just as music and stories do. Granted, each art form (and surely families are just as much a composition as are songs and folktales) is elusive, problematic, troubled, and troubling; but, taken together, they make us what we are. As Wideman puts it, in a passage about Art & Life worth quoting in its entirety:

> Stories are onions. You peel one skin and another grins up at you. And peeling onions can make grown men cry. Which raises other questions. Why does one transparent skin on top of another transparent skin, layer after layer you can see through if each is held up to the light, why are they opaque when bound one on top of the other to form an onion or story? Like a sentence with seven clear simple words and you understand each word but the meaning of the sentence totally eludes you. You might suggest there is no light source at the core of the onion, nothing similar to a lamp that can be switched on so you can see from outside in. Or you might say an onion is the light and the truth, or at least as much truth and light as you're ever going to receive on this earth, source and finished product all rounded into

> one and that's the beauty of solid objects you can hold in your hand. Each skin, each layer a different story, connected to the particular, actual onion you once held whole in your hand as the onion is connected to stars, dinosaurs, bicycles, a loon's cry, to the seed it sprouted from the earth where the seed rotted and died and slept until it began dreaming of being an onion again, dreamed the steps it would have to climb, the skins it would have to shed and grow to let its light shine again in the world.

Wideman is, of course, describing the curious way that the memories of *Fatheralong* interconnect; but at the same time he is suggesting, however unconsciously, how some stories remain stubbornly hidden beneath the layers. Thus far I have talked about the moose on the Wideman family dinner table as if it were restricted to Jake, the son both absent in fact and in story. But there is yet another moose on this table, for if *Fatheralong* ends with a poignant letter to that son ("I remember walking down towards the lake to be alone [on the day Wideman first heard that his son was missing and the boy sharing his room was dead] because I felt myself coming apart, the mask I'd been wearing, as much for myself as for the benefit of other people, was beginning to splinter. . . . I found myself on my knees, praying to a tree."), it begins with an impassioned plea for a raceless America, one in which color no longer "preempts our right to situate our story where we choose." Our power, Wideman argues, lies in the "capacity to imagine ourselves as other than what we are." Race, in short, is yet another hard reality Wideman prefers to ignore by wishing it away. Meanwhile, the moose on the table continues to stink.

I am hardly the only Wideman watcher who figured that *Fatheralong* would turn out to be at least as much about Wideman the father as it is about Wideman the son—not, I hope, for prurient interests or hundreds of other wrong reasons, but because I felt he could lead me past newspaper platitudes (senseless, sad, and the all-purpose "tragic") to a deeper understanding of the dark truths underlying much human behavior. I wondered too, if he would play the race card, and if so, which one; or if he would offer up an explanation I cannot even imagine, but that a genuine writer can. Perhaps Wideman is simply not ready to write such a book, at least not yet. In that case, he should have written about something else because his meditation about fathers and sons, race and society, turns out to be yet another look past the moose on the table. All of us, black and white, have had far too many of those.

Black Rage/White Guilt: Act II

Faces at the Bottom of the Well: The Permanence of Racism. By Derrick Bell. New York: Basic Books, 1992. 222 pp.

Confronting Authority: Reflections of an Ardent Protester. By Derrick Bell. Boston: Beacon Press, 1994. 195 pp. $20.00.

Tragedy, we are told, tends to repeat itself as farce; the same might be said for rage. As a staple ingredient of the modernist temperament, rage once sported an impressive pedigree: Nietzsche's Zarathustra, Dostoevsky's underground man, Ezra Pound's Hugh Selwyn Mauberley, and nearly any protagonist in a D. H. Lawrence novel. Taken together, these creations of the modernist imagination embody what the late Irving Howe called "an unyielding rage against the official order," one as much defined by everything their authors rejected as by what they embraced.

Modernist writing intended to be rigorously elitist, reserved not only for readers willing to grapple with its infuriating difficulties but also for cultural rebels eager to sample its attractive dangers. If the abyss that beckoned was filled with monsters at the bottom, it also promised the ultimate reward of a self-knowledge that the complacent would never share.

But if modernist rage was once the province of artists alternately blessed and cursed by visions of the New, rage of a decidedly lower order threatens to become our culture's common currency. The mass of men—and women—no longer live what Henry David Thoreau confidently believed were "lives of quiet desperation"; now they trot out their grievances (and the rage such accusations invariably produce) on AM talk radio and afternoon television shows hosted by the likes of Oprah, Sally Jesse Raphael, and Geraldo—and all this while intellectuals sputter and fume in what can only be called the very quiet desperation of symposia that even C-Span doesn't cover or in the pages of journals that couch potatoes never read.

Black rage is an important subdivision of this contemporary phenomenon, not only because it has a gripping force that the most sensationalistic TV fare finally lacks, but also because black rage has a cultural history against which we can judge its present incarnations. One could argue that *this* rage is nearly as old as the country itself, and certainly as old as the arrival of the first slave ships to our shores. What, after all, were the slave revolts and impassioned slave narratives but a rage against the existing order that had stripped away their humanity and reduced them—legally, physically, and spiritually—to chattel?

Nonetheless, let me suggest that the rage pulsing through many contemporary black narratives owes its largest debts to Richard Wright's *Native Son* (1940), a novel Irving Howe once described as having changed American culture forever:

> In all its crudeness, melodrama, and claustrophobia of vision, Richard Wright's novel brought into the open, as no one ever had before, the hatred, fear, and violence that have crippled and may yet destroy our culture. . . . A blow at the white man, the novel forced him to recognize himself as an oppressor. A blow at the black man, the novel forced him to recognize the cost of his submission.
>
> —from "Black Boys and Native Sons" (1963)

Native Son was, in short, *the* Negro novel that successive generations of black writers, understandably enough, would struggle against but never quite supplant, for it had put an awkward finger on the only problem worth writing about in the first place. "No American Negro exists," Baldwin would later admit, "who does not have his private Bigger Thomas living in his skull."

Let us admit that Howe rightly assessed the raw power of Wright's novel while also admitting that his formulation sells the black experience and the black imagination far too short. For if Bigger Thomas is simultaneously product and prophet of an America doomed to destruction, there is little to be done and even less to be said. In such a scenario, black rage and white guilt are destined to be locked in the death grip of our collective destiny.

In differing ways, both Baldwin and Ellison took issue with Howe's assessment. For Baldwin, the protest novel was a decidedly limited form, and many of his early essays (collected in

1961 in *Nobody Knows My Name*) were intended to question the stereotyping of blacks as social victims and mythic sexual animals. Was there not, Baldwin argued in seminal essays such "Everybody's Protest Novel" and "Many Thousands Gone," a richer, more artistically expansive way of transcending the narrow confines of naturalist fiction?

"The World and the Jug" (1964), Ellison's extended response to Howe's essay, went even further, accusing Howe of seeing Negroes as "abstract embodiments of living hell" rather than as fully human people; and, as a consequence, of utterly failing to see beyond the burden of blackness to the discipline those conditions inspire. There is, Ellison insisted, a fullness, a richness, in black life "*despite* the realities of politics."

As the cunning of history would have it, the magisterial debates occasioned by Howe's "Black Boys and Native Sons" were soon overshadowed by political cries for "Black Power!" and by the ways that impetus was given literary expression by the black aesthetic movement of the late 1960s and early 1970s. As Howe put it ruefully, "White literary intellectuals are often eager to declare an uncritical—which is, I think, patronizing—acceptance of Black Power ideology," one that, Howe correctly observed, "would dismiss both Ellison and me as old-fashioned, irrelevant, and—most shattering of blows!—'mere liberal' advocates of 'integration.'" No doubt Howe chafed when Ellison set about instructing him in the range and depth of black experience (Howe, after all, was always more comfortable on the "giving" end of lectures, and he must have been driven to apoplexy when Black Power ideologues made it abundantly clear that Whitey's words were no longer welcome, even (especially?) when they tripped off liberal Jewish tongues.

At the same time, however, I suspect that Ellison suffered deeper grief, because his noble words about the double-sidedness of the American experience sounded a conciliatory note out of joint with the times. Bad enough that *Invisible Man* was the trump card every black novelist had to beat for mainstream recognition or that whole paragraphs from Ellison's essays were dragged out and quoted by liberal white critics; worse, the black aesthetic movement made a case for a distinctive modus operandi that must have made Ellison shiver.

Black rage produced oceans of ink, and guilty white readers could not buy them quickly enough. What I have in mind are such nearly forgotten anthologies as William H. Grier and

Price M. Cobb's *Black Rage* (1968), LeRoi Jones and Larry Neal's *Black Fire* (1968) or Addison Gayle, Jr.'s *Black Expression* (1969)—all published at a time when black undergraduates sported Afros and clenched fists, and insisted that Black Studies programs (with appropriately separatist professors) be established immediately. Rage was the era's charged word, and if the arguments mounted on behalf of a black aesthetic movement sound familiar, it is because the words of Act I were simply dusted off a quarter-century later and offered up as Act II. Here, for example, is James T. Stewart, from an essay entitled "The Development of the Black Revolutionary Artist" (1963): ". . . we must emancipate our minds from Western values and standards. We must rid our minds of these values. Saying so will not be enough"; and here is Hoyt W. Fuller, from "Towards a Black Aesthetic" (1964):

> . . . the break between the revolutionary black writers and the "literary mainstream" is, perhaps of necessity, cleaner and more decisive than the noisier and more dramatic break between the black militants and the traditional political and institutional structures. Just as black intellectuals have rejected the NAACP on the one hand, and the two major political parties, on the other, and gone off in search of new and more effective means and methods of seizing power, so revolutionary black writers have turned their backs on the old "certainties" and struck out in new, if uncharted, directions. They have begun the journey toward a black aesthetic.

All this, of course, has a deeply American ring (however incongruous the observation, then and now, might seem), for nothing so characterizes our cultural history as an insistence on the New and Improved. Unfortunately, the black aesthetic movement largely defined itself in terms of opposition, by what it was *not* rather than by what it was. The result is that one reads manifesto after strident manifesto from the architects of the black aesthetic movement only to discover that writers are valued in direct proposition to their non-Western, non-mainstream, and indeed non-literary attributes. What their work expresses, however, often seems little more than its own inchoate rage. In this sense, the following lines—from LeRoi Jones's "Black Art"—are representative:

> . . . We want poems
> like fists beating niggers out of Jocks
> of dagger poems in the slimy bellies
> of the owner-Jews. . . .
> We want a black poem. And a
> Black World.

Let the world be a Black Poem
And Let All Black People Speak This Poem
Silently
or LOUD

Small wonder that the first incarnations of the black aesthetic movement fizzled; the marvel is that it should now have a new lease on life in writers who can once again capitalize on the reciprocal relationship between black rage and white guilt. Consider, for example, the recent spate of books—each widely reviewed and lavishly praised—that bid for our attention by way of the sheer rage they pack: Brent Staples's *Parallel Time: Growing Up in Black and White* (1994), Ellis Cose's *The Rage of the Privileged Class* (1993) and Nathan McCall's *Makes Me Wanna Holler* (1994). For Staples and McCall, the systematic pain of growing up black is all the evidence necessary to prove that whites and blacks live inside two quite different, mutually opposed worlds: racism provides the animus, and rage becomes a predictable response. Granted, these are books about how the respective authors managed to escape their predictable fates—both men became journalists on high-powered, important newspapers—but their stories still simmer with residual resentment.

By contrast, Ellis Cose's *The Rage of a Privileged Class* argues that behind the apparent trappings of success—Ivy League educations, six-figure incomes, palatial homes—lies the bitter reality of angry, disillusioned blacks. Rage, in short, is not confined to those trapped in the underclass and our inner cities, but is also alive and well among those who nightly cry themselves to sleep on silken pillows.

Enter Derrick Bell, a man once caught up in the civil Rights movement—first as a lawyer for the NAACP and then as the Harvard law school's first tenured black professor—but now a man who cannot recant his earlier life fast enough. He has seen the light, and what it shows him is the full dimensions of how he, and the Civil Rights struggle itself, have been had. "Racism," Bell insists, "is an integral, permanent, and indestructible component of this society." From the high moral ground that turned "We Shall Overcome" into an anthem uniting the most progressive elements of the black and white community, Bell offers up a new song, one that might go something like this: "We Can't Overcome, and, Moreover, We Never Could." True enough, when I imagine the words to this imaginary song I realize that Bell is simultaneously very close to and very far from the in-your-face posturing of rap groups like Public Enemy or Snoop Doggy Dog—close because his message is essentially separatist and self-defeating; far because Harvard types (black or white) are not especially known for their street smarts or natural rhythm.

Bell, in short, heaves himself into the racial divide armed with eloquence rather than ghetto slang and a custom-tailored $600 suit rather than a dashiki. Like most of us, he wears sunglasses to fend off glare, not because he wants to make an intimidating point. All of which makes *his* impassioned arguments worth taking seriously, for unlike the current wave of black demagogues, Bell directs his arguments to white liberals rather than crowds of the desperate and downtrodden. But make no mistake, his orderly, even elegant prose is out to push the same militantly separatist agenda.

Bell knows full well that "teaching the white folk" is at once a manifestation of faith and an exercise in folly. His late wife Jewel constantly reminded him about the latter, gently counseling her impassioned spouse that he "was not necessarily doing 'good,'" that the road to bruised feelings and misunderstanding was often paved with noble intentions. Such a moment—more revealing than Bell may realize—occurred when he gave a reading from *Faces at the Bottom of the Well* at a Washington, D.C. bookstore. As Bell describes the incident (in the Preface to the book's paperback edition), a well-dressed, articulate black woman listened to his litany of hopelessness and then challenged his assumptions this way: "Professor Bell, you have achieved much despite racial discrimination. How dare you now deny our children the hope that they may enjoy a success like yours?" Bell responded by claiming that she had confused the messenger with the message, that he "simply chronicled what society had done and was likely to do." My hunch is that Bell would not be prepared to extend the same rationale to the argument Charles Murray and Richard J. Herrnstein advance in *The Bell Curve*. Indeed, the plot thickens at this point because Murray and Herrnstein buttress their controversial study of I.Q. and social consequences with the stuff of science—statistics, charts, graphs—while Bell depends largely on anecdotal evidence and gut feelings. Murray and Herrnstein argue that it's time to "get real" about how hopeless Head Start programs are when directed toward those with low I.Q.'s; Bell feels that it is high time whites and blacks skim their eyes and see the hard truths about American racism for what they are. Different folks, different strokes, but both parties end up advancing positions that are deeply wrong.

Bell's point is two-fold and seemingly contradictory: on one hand, racism is a permanent part of the American landscape; on the other, the "obligation to try and improve the lots of blacks and other victims of injustice (including whites) does not end because final victory over racism is unlikely, even impossible." The result, Bell goes on to argue, is a formula both realistic and satisfying, for "the essence of a life fulfilled—a succession of actions undertaken in righteous causes—is a victory in itself."

The rub is that Bell is so focused on the failures of the Civil Rights Movement that he fails to acknowledge its considerable successes. By any measure, blacks have made enormous strides since the 1950s—to check this out all Bell need do is take a plane to virtually any city in the Deep South—but he prefers to think of integration and its tangible fruits (everything from the eradication of Jim Crow laws to a burgeoning black middle class) as "*temporary 'peaks of progress,'*" extended to blacks by powerful whites and prompted not by evidences of good will, but by a covert racism more insidious than its older forms.

Moreover, Bell is convinced that even small gains are doomed to "*slide into irrelevance as racial patterns adapt in ways that maintain white dominance.*" This gloomy conclusion, Bell tells us, is verified by "history," although the evidentiary record—the footnotes, if you will—of this truth are noticeably absent in his book. Rather, what Bell offers up in *Faces From the Bottom of the Well* are moral fables, some prompted by his resident Muse, the lawyer-prophet Geneva Crenshaw of Bell's *And We Are Not Saved: The Elusive Quest for Racial Justice* (1987), others by discussions with a cab driver named Jesse B. Semple (yes, *that* Mr. Semple, the one we associate with Langston Hughes).

Bell's allegories will never be confused with those of Nathaniel Hawthorne, so he would be well advised to keep his day job (currently, as visiting professor at New York University), but what finally matters is the force of his arguments and not the niceties of his fiction. Bell has a hankering for the supernatural, and in tales such as "The Afroantica Awakening" and "The Space Traders," he causes mythical lands to pop up from the ocean or aliens to drop in from outer space. At their best, they are likely to prompt as much serious discussion as outrage. In

"The Space Traders," arguably the best of the lot, aliens propose a devil's bargain—America's blacks for much-needed gold and extraterrestrial technology. One can only cringe at how such a swap would play out on talk radio. And while Bell does his best to represent those constituencies that would oppose the deal, the fantasy ends, as it must, with America's blacks once again in shackles and bound for yet another middle passage.

Does Bell imagine that such a vision is likely, much less true? Of course not, but it does rather sharpen his focus on an America that vacillates between schemes to "disappear" its blacks and conspiratorial methods of keeping them down. With "A Law Professor's Protest," in which the president of Harvard and all one hundred and sixty-nine of its black professors are blown up in an explosion, America's racist highway leads to 17 Quincy Street, Cambridge, Massachusetts. Fantasy—here thinly disguised as a bizarre wish projection—sets the scene for what would otherwise be an essay exploring how it is that Harvard continues to drag its heels on affirmative action, despite what looks for all the world like solid progress.

Indeed, *protest* is the charged word of Bell's newest incarnation, for whatever may be said about his accomplishments as a steady worker in the civil rights struggles, or about his years as a Harvard Law School professor, what defines him is his unsuccessful struggle to make the law school do the right thing by hiring a black female, and the heavy costs he subsequently paid. *Confronting Authority* is Bell's side of this sad story, one in which an institution refused to blink—insisting that no exception be made to its leave-of-absence policy—and a protester ended up getting the sack.

Bell pleads his (special) case, arguing that if Harvard had been interested in retaining his services, its hard-and-fast rules could have been bent. No matter that the same policy—and result—was applied to the likes of Henry Kissinger when he opted to serve Nixon rather than Harvard. No matter that many who praised Bell in public whispered about the quality of his legal scholarship in private. No matter that Bell himself was not above encouraging—some would say, manipulating—his black law students to boycott their exams, first to further the cause of minority hiring and then to show support for Bell himself. No matter that his was a case of competing visions and widely differing notions of hiring criteria. For Bell, what the sorry debacle boiled down to was an intransigent racism masquerading as high standards:

> The standards for hiring and promoting faculty at Harvard Law School (and in fairness, at almost every major law school in the country) erect almost unassailable barriers of class and race. Bearing little correlation to effective teaching or significant scholarship, the criteria's most uniform effect is to produce a group of law professors whose backgrounds, education, interests, and writing most closely resemble those of the wealthy white men who have dominated law faculties from the beginning.

Confronting Authority is the saga of how Bell martyred himself for beliefs some will call noble and others will find badly deluded. If he remains surprised that Harvard made him pony up for his protest (even a casual reading of Thoreau's "Civil Disobedience" could have enlightened him on this point), he is even more shocked by the way close friends wrote off his action as foolish. Small wonder, then, that Bell's treatise writ in exile strikes such a self-righteous note. For he did not merely insist that the law school tenure a woman of color; more important, she was one who was not white under the skin. "The goal of diversity," he told a student rally, "will not be served by persons who look black and think white."

In Bell's case, it is but a short step from racial certainty (he alone presumably defines what being and thinking black means) to a rage he mollifies by calling it liberation: "As the saying goes, in order to free the body, one must first free the mind. Those who value themselves will have the courage and sense of self-worth to demand to be treated fairly and respectfully."

One could argue that Bell was, in fact, treated fairly (the rules applying to everyone else applied to him) and that Harvard accorded him the full respect it grants to other faculty members. What Harvard did *not* do was agree with his protest, and I, for one, do not equate disagreement with racism, institutional or otherwise. Bell believes—indeed, he *must* believe—that a commitment to change requires that one confront authority, not because you will always win, and not even because you will always be right, but because "your faith in what you believe is right must be a living, working faith, a faith that draws you away from comfort and security and toward risk, when necessary, through confrontation." If the facts matched his rhetoric, the result would have been noble words for a sad occasion—namely, Bell's farewell speech to his former law students. What seeps through, however, are not only large measures of self-justification, but also newer, more insidious versions of black rage.

Bell is hardly alone in tossing the race card onto the public table, but he is notable for the way he has moved a separatist agenda from street corners and little "little magazines" to our elitist law schools. Moreover, his argument—that racism is the tattoo on every black American's skin—offers succor to those who could not care a fig about what happens at Harvard. For them, Bell's "racism-as-tattoo" excuses any cases of black pathology and cancels any gains that most blacks justifiably view with pride.

Black rage is finally as much a strategy as a condition, and in terms of sheer escalation it now threatens to join cries about "Wolf!" and "The sky is falling down" as phrases so overused that they lose whatever force they originally had. In an important 1988 essay entitled "The Rage of Race," the social critic Stanley Crouch points out that we should not be particularly surprised, for rage is the province of a people who have been "led up paths that resulted in imprisonment, spiritual collapse, and death for goals far less logical than acquiring political power through inclusion into the social contract." Derrick Bell, by giving confrontation and protest the spin he does, emerges as yet another figure who offers solutions as simple-minded and dangerous as those that clogged the bookstores during the 1960s—an age that seems at once, long ago and just like yesterday.

One by One From the Inside Out: Essays and Reviews on Race and Responsibility in America. By Glenn C. Loury. New York: Free Press, 1995. 332 pp. $25.00.

Glenn C. Loury's first book, a cobbling of eleven essays and thirteen reviews, is noteworthy not only because it is his *first* book, but also because it arrives on the heels of a *New Yorker* profile (May 2, 1995), that spared no punches about the private demons that once raged inside Loury's very conflicted psyche. By day, he fairly dripped with Success; a tenured economics professor at Harvard at the tender age of thirty-four, the world—or at least the part of it that public intellectuals control—was his oyster. *Commentary* magazine gladly printed his no-nonsense critiques of affirmative action policy, the Reagan administration groomed him for an important cabinet post, and Loury soon acquired that elusive entity most American intellectuals [secretly] crave: a Big Rep. As a very conspicuous black conservative, Loury was simultaneously lauded and reviled, courted by some and shunned by others. All this, as it were, constituted the Loury one encountered on talk shows, prestigious symposia, and in the pages of the *New York Times*.

But there was a very different Loury *bi nacht*—this one given to haunting Boston's underbelly in search of drugs, booze, and illicit sex. To say that this Loury was an embarrassment to his neoconservative boosters would be to put the matter charitably, for the same Loury who argued—with eloquence and great forcefulness—that inner-city blacks needed to clean up their acts was headed toward a very public crack up.

Not surprisingly, he reaped the bitter disappointments he had sown: he withdrew his nomination as Deputy Secretary of Education; and with his marriage in near shambles, enrolled in a drug rehabilitation center. Even more important, perhaps, Loury virtually dropped out as a public intellectual who had made race relations in America his special beat. The irony, of course, is that being black and smart had been at once Loury's blessing and his curse—for the same pressures that bind young black men to the 'hood (where narrow definitions of "blackness" are rigorously, often ruthlessly, enforced) had shackles long enough to reach inside Ivy League walls. Put another way, it was not merely Loury's reservations about affirmative action that raised eyebrows, but, rather, that he had made his way into "the white man's world." No matter that combinations of brains, hard work, and the luck of cultural timing had a good deal to do with Loury's spectacular rise; to those blacks he left behind, he was a traitor, a person trying to "pass."

The writings collected in *One by One From the Inside Out* provide Loury with an opportunity to talk about his personal situation as well as the larger ramifications it points toward. For if group definition becomes the sole measure of individual worth, the result can only lead to the pathologies that end in self destruction. Loury's account of his long dark night of the soul and subsequent recovery is an eloquent testimony to the therapeutic value of faith (as he puts it in the book's final line, "No Jesus, no peace.") as well as an unflinching reminder of just how powerful the pressures to be blacker-than-thou, in fact, are:

> I no longer believe that the camaraderie engendered among blacks by our collective experience of racism constitutes an adequate basis for any person's self-definition. Even if I restrict attention to the question "Who am I as a black American at the end of the twentieth century?" these considerations of historical victimization and struggle against injustice do not take me very far toward finding an answer. I am made "black" only in the most superficial way by being the object of a white racist's hate. The empathetic exchange of survivors' tales among "brothers," even the collective struggle against the clear wrong of racism, does not provide a tableau sufficiently rich to give meaning and definition to the totality of my life. I am so much more than the one wronged, misunderstood, underestimated, derided, or ignored by whites. I am more than the one who has struggled against this oppression and indifference; more than a descendant of slaves now claiming freedom; more, that is, than either a "colored person" (as seen by the racist) or a "person of color" (as seen by the anti-racist).

Nor will the old political labels or alliances any longer work—whether they be Democratic or Republican, militant Leftist or doctrinaire neoconservative. For one thing, the world after the salad days of the Civil Rights Movement has become far too fluid for such certainties; for another, Loury himself is far more complicated than any single definition will allow for.

All of which brings us to the essay that many Jewish-American readers will find especially troubling: "The End of an Illusion: Black-Jewish Relations in the Nineties." In it, Loury makes no bones about the sour prospects for rekindling the spirit that once linked blacks and Jews in common cause. Wishful thinking aside, the bald truth—as Loury sees it—in that the old alliance of blacks and Jews has ruptured beyond repair, and that visions of what America is (and the politics that these visions engender) now deeply divides us. In short, "relations between American blacks and Jews are clearly in deep trouble"; and they are likely to get worse, rather than better, in the foreseeable future.

Why so? Because the struggle now is for power, and in that struggle about reparations for slavery, affirmative action, quotas, a wide umbrella of entitlements and social programs on one hand and the principle of meritocracy on the other, blacks and Jews bring radically differing histories and perceptions to the table. Thus,

> . . . in the decades since the enactment of the great civil rights laws, the goals that blacks and Jews have sought to attain through political activity diverged. More importantly, the principled commitments—the ideals and beliefs that animate and inform public action by members of the groups—have also grown far apart. Ultimately it is this conflict of public visions between the black and Jewish political elites that lies behind the current difficulties. The conflict of visions, about the nature of American society and the role of its governing structures in promoting the welfare of its citizens, is now so severe as to preclude a restoration of the historic cooperative relationship between the groups.

This much said, however, Loury hastens to add that he is not thinking about extremist positions—either those advocated by the Nation of Islam or the Jewish Defense League—but, rather, about the respectable, mainstream agendas on both sides. Granted, a considerable number of liberal Jews remain, those more than willing to vote *against* the interests of their pocketbooks, but they are a dwindling band. Jews are now able to voice what was once unthinkable—namely, that perhaps it is time to admit that the "love" has gone out of this marriage, and the prospect of divorce, however saddening, must be considered. Indeed, that is Loury's view as well, partly because he feels that blacks might forge their own future by way of what he calls "Christian nationalism" (his alternative to the self-empowerment programs of Minister Louis Farrakhan) and partly because he believes that what blacks and Jews rightly share is the special fundamentalism of their respective faith communities. We can, in short, meet in prayer, but not any longer in political rallies. Those days are long gone, and it is high time for both groups to have an end to the illusion that they will likely return.

The other essays in Loury's collection are equally provocative, touching on his prescriptions for black dignity, black progress, and how best to end black economic discrimination. As for his reviews, they have insightful things to say about important books such as Cornel West's *Race Matters*, Andrew Hacker's *Two Nations*, Stephen L. Carter's *Reflections of an Affirmation Action Baby*, Shelby Steele's *The Content of Our Character*, and Richard J. Herrnstein and Charles Murray's *The Bell Curve*, but they tell us even more about Loury himself. There is little question that race is a hot topic for those in the book-publishing business, but in this crowded field, Loury's collection stands both tall and important. Faith has clearly constituted Loury's personal salvation, and for that, we can all rejoice. Whether it can translate into an enlightened, effective public policy is, however, quite another matter. But one thing is clear: we have gone about as far down the road of hatred and divisiveness as a democracy dare go.